UNCIVIL WAR:
AMERICAN VOICES

LaTonda Evette McQueen & April Jones Daugherty

DAUGHERTY
& MCQUEEN
publishing

First paperback edition April 2021.

Cover images by Torrance Reed. (@Blacktiger_art)
Internal images by April Jones Daugherty.

ISBN 978-1-7369468-0-0 (paperback)

Published by Daugherty & McQueen Publishing. (Send all inquiries via email DaQueenPublishing@gmail.com)

Scripture quotations marked MSG are taken from THE MESSAGE, copyright © 1993, 2002, 2018 by Eugene H. Peterson. Used by permission of NavPress, represented by Tyndale House Publishers. All rights reserved.

Scripture quotations marked ESV are from the ESV® Bible (The Holy Bible, English Standard Version®), copyright © 2001 by Crossway Bibles, a publishing ministry of Good News Publishers. Used by permission. All rights reserved.

UNCIVIL WAR

Aliyah (May 2020)

I read what they say,
but I can't learn to hear it.
Uncivil, unrestrained,
opinions flame, foundations split.
As the ghost of America
haunts States un-United,
this war we're finishing burns,
but for the dying, we must keep fighting.

For our children, our heroes.

Contents

About the Book

Our Why

2020 burned.
Everything and in every way.
There were witnesses, victims, and participants at play.
Many of us were all of these on any given day.
Pieces of the lives we had,
or the lives we thought we had,
or the ones we longed to have,
scattered all over the ground—
none of them fitting together.

What could we do?
Amid the tragedy, such casualties,
what could anyone do?
All these dreams with jagged edges,
singed and tired consequences?
For us sister-friends, poets, and mothers,
teachers, and always students of others,
we knew we could listen.
We knew we could search for pieces together.

We also knew _we could write_.
And we did. _All day. All night._
We wrote the emotions, the pain, _and_ the light
2020 both created, unearthed, and changed.
We wrote the raging flames,
the voices of strength, loss, Hope and Hate.
We gathered the pieces,
so many pieces,
and widened the lens, trying to see and show them all at once.

And some things fit.
Jagged pieces, to others knit.
While other pieces would not quit,
rubbing, breaking, until edges lit
more fires, more making of pieces—
all of them scattered on the ground like fragile ash.
We could not gather the pieces fast enough, the task too rough.
The voices, like flames, burning our throats and fingers,
as we wove words and pieces, stories and lives, together.

Until at last we stopped.
Covered in soot, sweat, tears, and chalks,
we stood back and beheld, through the wide lens of our art,
flames that had fought to be raised, to be heard,
flames that could do *more* than burn:
Flames that could teach, empathy learned.
Voices that could speak, sing, pray, and discern a soul to a new place, a
    forgotten place.
Voices that could open eyes to a better dream. We saw Black voices raised—
high, out of the ash. Flames of light that gleam. Heard and shining.

We also saw the hope of new voices:
Black and White, lifted and listening, making new choices.
We saw sparks of hope in conversations,
as you and yours waded into the flames of *Uncivil War: American Voices*.
Then you let these voices of flame and heat reach your heart...
    ...and we saw a spark, a place to start...
Hate damned by the weary willing to wage war within themselves and within
    the world.
For a nation's soul. For Justice. For *every* Black boy and girl.
It was what we had come to do.
    It is what we could do,
        so we did.

Characters

Uncivil War: American Voices is a collection of voices speaking in verse. Out of passion and pain, and in conversation with one another, these voices tell the story of racial injustice in America.

All of our characters live in Houston, Texas, in the year 2020. While the pandemic is a thread running necessarily through this book, it is not the focus of the voices within it. Instead, *Uncivil War: American Voices* invites you to engage with the lived experiences and warring opinions surrounding the racial injustice spotlighted by the year's events.

These are their voices:

Aliyah—A Black woman in her late twenties, Aliyah is the weekday manager at Jack's Bar and Grill. Aliyah is dating Darius and is Imani's niece. Aliyah has labored as an activist for social justice for most of her adult years, long before the events of 2020.

America—This voice is a collective cry from all Americans. It only appears once in *Uncivil War: American Voices*. We are so broken and divided as a nation that it is remarkable our collective cries could be unified at all.

Belinda—A Black woman of any age who does not support Black Lives Matter. This voice is not prominent in the Black community, so it is not featured heavily in this book. This voice is included, however, because not all Black people think, march, or vote alike, just as not all White people think, march, or vote alike. This cannot and should not be forgotten.

Brothers—When a diverse group of Black male voices speak within one poem, Brothers is used.

Darius—A Black man in his early thirties, Darius is the bartender at Jack's Bar and Grill. He is also taking courses at the University of Houston. Darius is dating Aliyah, whom he met through work. Darius grew up in the same neighborhood as Ty and has known Ty all his life. Darius also attended school with Kate in his last two years of high school, and they are old friends.

Dr.—A physician in his forties who treats Covid-19 patients in Houston's Medical Center. Dr. is an outside voice speaking into the chaos affecting all of our characters.

Gretchen—A White woman in her late thirties, Gretchen is an accountant for a small, local business. Gretchen is married to Nancy's son, Michael.[1] Gretchen, Michael, and Will grew up together, attending the same church and school. The three of them remain friends. Gretchen and Michael are still members of their childhood church.

J.R.—A White man in his early sixties, J.R. is a businessman, working in Houston's energy sector. J.R. is a frequent customer at Jack's and usually sits at the bar where Darius is the bartender.

Hate—A White man or woman of any age with hate in his/her heart. We did not want to give Hate any name that might disguise Hate as anything else. While we did not desire to elevate Hate's voice, we also could not leave Hate out.

Imani—A Black woman who is forty, Imani is an artist who works for a design firm in Houston. Imani is a frequent customer at Jack's with a personal connection to several of our characters. Imani attends church with Shawna. Imani is Aliyah's aunt, and Imani is one of Kate's closest friends. Some of Imani's art also appears within the book.

Kate—A White woman in her early thirties, Kate is a stay-at-home mother of young children. Kate is Will's wife and one of Imani's closest friends. Kate went to school with Darius, and they are old friends.

Mama—A Black mother whose son was wrongly killed by police. Mama is every mama of every Black victim of racial violence. She is also one Mama of one victim: Son, a young man several of our characters knew and loved. Mama lost Son long before 2020, but she feels his loss all over again in this tumultuous year. Mama is "Mama" because her name, and so many mamas' names, are not known. Son is "Son" because his name, and so many sons' and daughters' names, are not known.

Nancy—A White woman in her early sixties, Nancy works as a secretary in a law office across the street from Jack's. Nancy often lunches at the restaurant during the week. Nancy attends church with her son Michael and her daughter-in-law Gretchen.

Shawna—A Black woman in her forties, Shawna is the owner of Jack's Bar and Grill, where most of our characters either work or dine. Shawna is recently widowed. Her husband Jack died from cancer two years ago. Shawna and Jack opened the restaurant together. Son worked there. Aliyah, Will, and Darius still work there.

---

[1] Michael does not speak in this book, although he is mentioned and does connect several characters to one another.

Several of our other characters frequent the restaurant—or did until Covid-19 descended on Houston in March of 2020. Shawna is also a mother to a son and daughter.[2]

Silent Right—A large group of White Republicans of any age who do not have a prominent voice within this work because they often choose to not speak. While the Silent Right does not often engage in discussions about race in America, their silence speaks volumes. Within this book, the Silent Right's contribution is limited to expressing their desire to be left out of it.

Sisters—When a diverse group of Black female voices speak within one poem, Sisters is used.

Ty—A Black man in his mid-twenties, Ty works as a driver for a parcel delivery service. Ty delivers packages to the restaurant, as well as to the neighborhood and businesses near the restaurant. Ty's route includes the office where Nancy works, Shawna's house, and Nancy's house. Ty grew up in the same neighborhood as Darius.

Will—A White man in his late thirties, Will is the weeknight and weekend manager at Jack's Bar and Grill. Will is married to Kate, and they have children. Will also grew up with Gretchen (and Gretchen's husband, Michael), in both school and church. Will no longer attends the church they all grew up attending. He and Kate attend a newer church in downtown Houston.

---

[2] Both Shawna and Kate have poems where they are speaking with their children. Their children call them Mama. Do not confuse these instances with the character Mama.

Character Connections

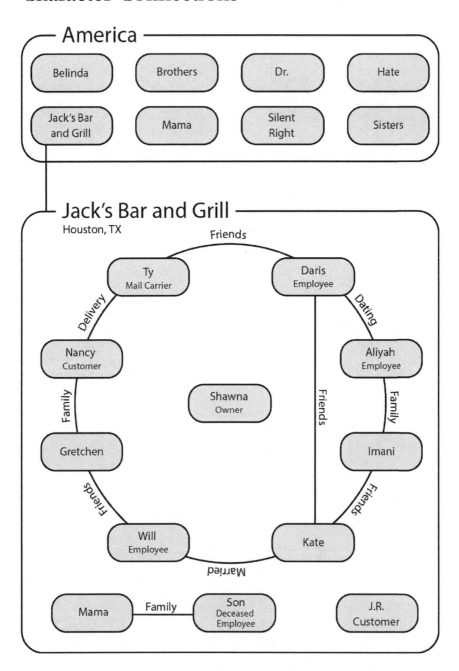

America

- Belinda
- Brothers
- Dr.
- Hate
- Jack's Bar and Grill
- Mama
- Silent Right
- Sisters

Jack's Bar and Grill

Houston, TX

- Ty — Mail Carrier
- Daris — Employee
- Nancy — Customer
- Aliyah — Employee
- Shawna — Owner
- Gretchen
- Imani
- Will — Employee
- Kate
- Mama
- Son — Deceased Employee
- J.R. — Customer

Friends — Ty / Daris
Delivery — Ty / Nancy
Dating — Daris / Aliyah
Family — Nancy / Gretchen
Family — Aliyah / Imani
Friends — Daris / Kate
Friends — Gretchen / Will
Friends — Imani / Kate
Married — Will / Kate
Family — Mama / Son

Prelude

I Cannot Breathe!

America (March 15, 2020 – May 24, 2020, Covid-19 begins to spread across the country, in-person school is suspended, and most of the country is in a lockdown of one kind or another. George Floyd is alive. Few know his name.)

Heavy.
Is the weight pressing on my neck?
Is the weight around my feet?
Is the weight sitting on my chest?
I cannot breathe!
I cannot breathe!

Am I the doctor who holds her hand?
Am I the widower who drowns in grief?
Am I the patient whose fever spikes?
I cannot breathe!
I cannot breathe!

Am I the mother who schools from home?
Am I the father my kids can't see?
Am I the worker who's lost my job?
I cannot breathe!
I cannot breathe!

Heavy.
Is the weight pressing on my neck.
Is the weight around my feet.
Is the weight sitting on my chest.
I cannot breathe!
I cannot breathe!

This poem was written *before* March 25, 2020, the day George Floyd—an unarmed Black man with Covid-19—was excruciatingly suffocated by the knee of a White police officer on American soil. It was written before Floyd's words, "I can't breathe"—words he was not the first Black man to utter; words bolstered and lifted high by the collective, dying words of so many Black men and women before him—became famous and lamented all over the world. The words of this poem were inscribed on our history and on America's weary hearts long before Floyd's immortal words were ever brandished on signs and marched through our streets.

But that is why we heard them.

A Single Match

There Was a Death Today

Shawna (May 25, 2020, A conversation with her son, the day a nation watched George Floyd murdered.)

I heard there was a death today,
Mama.
A Black man was handcuffed,
Mama.
His face was on the ground,
Mama.
The policeman was on his neck,
Mama.
And he said, "I can't breathe,"
Mama.
He called out for his **mama**,
Mama.
Why?

Mama sighed,
And held back tears
As she pondered how to answer her **son**.
The weight of the worry etched on her face,
As she knelt down to him.
She placed her hand on his head
And rubbed the tears from his eyes.

Yes, a man died today,
Son.
Yes, he was handcuffed,
Son.
His face was on the ground,
Son.
The policeman was on his neck,
Son.
Yes, he said "I can't breathe",
Son.
He called out for his **mama**,
Son.
He called out to God,
Son.
God heard him but the officer ignored him,

Son.
I don't know why.

Wrapped in his **mama's** arms,
Son was safe.
Mama wiped a tear
That escaped her tightly closed eyes.
Wondering when her beautiful Black boy
Would become the feared
BIG, BLACK MAN.
Mama wasn't ready for
The world
To see her **son** as
The darkness.
When all she saw was light.
Not ready to hear
"I can't breathe, **Mama**."

Fires

Revolt

Ty (May 28, 2020)

Stop calling me a riot.
>   *Call me a revolution*.
Stop calling me defiant.
>   *Call me the last solution*.
On oppression you're reliant.
>   *I'll tear down your institutions*.
On repentance you go quiet.
>   *I'll take back my restitution*.

Concrete

Aliyah

Concrete,
You know of tears.
You know of muffled cries
And knees buckled
Under the weight
Of Blackness.
You know of a beating
Heart stopping
And the chill as
Warmth leaves
It's impassioned
Plea of equity
And equality.

Concrete,
You know of tears.
You know the ache of a
Mama who drops to her knees.
You know of her
Wails to the wind;
A soul-piercing lullaby
To a child
Immortalized by a
Collective pain
And a hollowed sigh.
You know
Pain
And privilege.

Concrete,
You know of crowds
Marching, chanting, kneeling
As the weight of
Enough
And too much bear down
On a community.
You know of anger,
Long overdue

Shaking a foundation
Of chains
And cotton.
And color.

Concrete,
You know of patience
Of which we have no more.
You know of denial
And heads dipped
To ignore
The outstretched arms
Broken bodies
Blood and tears.
Concrete,
All this you know,
Yet whispered to
The Privileged.

Concrete,
It's time!
Concrete!
In your wisdom
Let them see.
Let them know.
Let them hear.
Let them kneel.
Let them join.
Let them wail.
Let us
Heal.

Masks

Darius

If you won't mask your freedom,
I will not mask my rage.
If you'll riot to mask your root-line,
I will riot to unmask our cage.
If you'll mask truth with patriotism,
I'll unmask truth in these streets.
If you'll mask supremacy as blessing,
I'll unmask America's lying Dream.
If you won't unmask your faithlessness,
I will unmask MY God—
    MY Moses, MY Elijah, MY Jesus—
    PROTESTING IN THESE STREETS WITH US!

Out of My Way

J.R.

I'm so tired of all the complaining.
Taking our President's name in vain, just sayin'.
Have some respect for yourself and country,
looting and shooting and begging for money.
Get out and work and earn like my daddy!
It's the land of the free, not incessantly chatty.
Talk is cheap if we're gonna be great again.
Need a President to shoot us straight. Amen!
I'll never vote for your liberal liars.
Where's the racism when you're settin' the fires?
Block my interstate, my streets, in your masks—
best be prayed up, 'cause I'm drivin' in fast.

Are We Interrupting Your Morning Commute?

Darius

Is it too much to ask for your stillness?
For interruption have you no resilience?
I've heard you complain about all the looting,
promising looting's just asking for shooting.
Yet when we peacefully protest oppression,
you're too inconvenienced to realize the lesson.
No matter the form our protest will take,
you'll interrupt it, you'll silence, unchanged.

23

How Do You Mourn

Shawna

How do you mourn someone you don't know?
Whose death haunts you from a hashtag or a video?
Whose cries of "I can't breathe!"
Echoed the pain of generations
As past names and faces
Scrolled across the screen.
Are they victims, heroes, or just casualties
Of a system that ignores the Black heartbreak and tears,
But cashes in on the privileged fears?
Pointing fingers at the response and rage
When the riots take center stage.

How do you mourn a face on the screen
And the face is all but forgotten, unseen?
When all the details emerge
And you see a community on the verge
Of destruction,
Of revolution,
From a problem with no solution?
At least not one of consensus,
But maybe of vengeance
After years of unheard cries
And breathless goodbyes.

How do you mourn this end?

No Fucks to Give

Ty

So, another Black man is dead
In these here streets.
Screamed and begged for his life
Underneath that cop's feet.
"Check his breathing!" someone cried.
Executed before being tried,
That man wanted to live.
But for a Black man
They had no fucks to give.

Big, Black, guilty,
Dangerous, and criminal
Are the first things they'll see.
Hell, I been told all my life
Gotta have my hands high, where they'll be seen.
Raised, on the dashboard, in cuffs—
Nah, ain't shit in them. But they won't believe.
Bullets gon' fly 'cause they got
No fucks to give for a Black man like me.

Death

Dr.

I'm not a man of faith. I'm a man of science.
But science has limits I never saw.
Like how half a nation can believe that I am lying.
My patients are dying, yet somehow, *I'm* wrong?

Just weeks ago, there were crowds, in the streets,
protesting the masks and restrictions that save their lives.
So, it'll be me, bearing the risk of their freedom.
Because of their foolishness, I risk son and wife.

I took an oath, so I will not forsake my patients.
But my patience for their insanity has run out.
Very few facts are truly relative and unsupported.
Instead of conspiracy, now it's science they doubt?

Just days ago, there was another man who could not breathe.
He needed a doctor, not a knee on his neck.
But we've sucked the very air out of the atmosphere of this country!
The only language we seem to speak here is that of death.

And now the streets are, once again, filling with people,
anguished anger, Covid, rubber bullets, and tear gas.
Too many enemies to count, though I too, must join in this fighting.
In this uncivil war, can my soul, can my stamina outlast?

Choosing My Words

Will

Should I be shocked?
Awed?
Certainly not appalled.
Their shouts were a long time coming.
Blacks have been silenced for far too long.
Yet the response,
from the brownstones
(so sure that this is overblown),
is dismissive and callous at best.
Looting confirms what they've always known.
And I feel tired,
already.
Yet in this fight, I will have to be steady.
Though it disgusts me, I know they might listen,
to "one of their own," otherwise they're unready.
Yet it's hard to pull back,
not speak,
words I desperately want to unleash.
Instead, I must weigh what might actually pierce
their walls of uprightness, blocking what they won't see.
So, I'm focused on Jesus,
his actions,
how he dined with the lowliest factions.
If there is one voice they've been trained to hear,
it's the King of a kingdom they've forgotten
amid distractions.
Should you read your Bible?
Sure!
But let me ask, is your sacrifice pure?
Because I see your two coats there,
as their voices tremble.
It's their oppression, not our ease, Christ endured.

Protest

J.R., Aliyah

J.R.

I protest your protest.
You have no cause, to take up your cause.
I protest your protest.
You challenge the law; we'll bring the law.
I protest your protest.
You handout masks, 'cause you live by handouts.
I protest your protest.
You stand out in streets, 'cause you need to stand out.
I protest your protest.
You march for black lives, but all lives matter.
I protest your protest.
You shatter our storefronts; your freedom will shatter.
I protest your protest.
You want reparations? What wrongs need repair?
I protest your protest.
You whine of unfairness; we've been more than fair.

Aliyah

You protest my protest?
You don't open your ears, let alone your eyes.
You protest my protest?
You act out of fear, believe right-wing lies.
You protest my protest?
How dare you name me, un-American thug.
You protest my protest?
Land of the free? Shit, enough is enough!
You protest my protest?
I protest your privilege, your hate, and your pride.
You protest my protest?
I'm not here to pillage, but I'll be damned if I'll hide.
You protest my protest?
That's just too bad, because I won't be silenced.
You protest *my* protest????
Yes, my Black body's mad, and it protests your violence.

Tell Me What I'm Supposed to Believe

Gretchen

Am I supposed to understand this?
Am I supposed to cheer for some revolution?
Am I supposed to rejoice at new revelations?
Am I supposed to protest a protest, or join in a protest?
Am I supposed to call myself privileged? Is it still OK to be White?
Am I supposed to decide to be an ally? Is that even allowed?
Am I supposed to just not be racist? Or is that not enough?
Am I supposed to be silent and let others speak? Or should I use my voice?
Am I supposed to fear the fires in the streets or marvel at their choice?
Am I supposed to have any fucking clue what constitutes freedom anymore?
Am I supposed to say fuck?
Am I supposed to wear a mask? Or protest one?
Am I supposed to still be frightened of Covid, or is that over?
Am I supposed to vote Democrat now, or can I still vote Republican?
Am I supposed to care about racist policies only, or can I care about other things?
Am I supposed to believe a word of what I hear in the news? Or tune it out?
Am I supposed to believe in anything anymore at all?
Am I supposed to have hope? Or…
Am I supposed to believe this is the beginning of the end and just accept it?
Because I certainly cannot be expected to understand this.

Mouths to Feed

Shawna

I've got mouths to feed.
Family
And employees,
Restaurant patrons who don't need
To sit inside and breathe
Poisoned air.

I've got mouths to feed.
Dough to knead,
Jack's memory to keep,
Here where we built our dream,
And it's all on me
To be fair.

I've got mouths to feed.
Under siege,
High taxed property,
Break even I'd be happy.
A livin' and our lives we need,
For much I care.

I've got mouths to feed.
Revolutionaries'
Marching feet—
What words can help them believe
Change is within reach,
When we're not there?

I've got mouths to feed.
Ain't no time to think,
No empty space to speak,
Just people who depend on me.
Decisions to swim or sink.
Can I bear
All these mouths to feed?

Mud

Hate

Black like mud.
Black ain't beautiful.
Black like darkness.
Black like evil.
Black is wrong.

But I can't say it.
Not out loud.

White like clean.
White is beautiful.
White like light.
White like godliness.
White is right.

But I can't say it.
Not out loud.

Damn niggers!
They know it's true.
That's why they tyin' my tongue.
That's why they're so angry.

Well I'll tie their hands!
Behind their backs.
Face in the mud—
Black like mud.
Now that's justice.

Yes, Sir, We Kneel

Darius

Yes Sir, no Sir.
Three bags full, Sir.
Of anger, pain, and pride, Sir.
May we move our hand, Sir?
May we take a stand, Sir?
May we kneel?
May we feel
Like the country we were brought to,
Bought to,
Fought for,
Died for
Is in a state that we pray for?
May we point out her faults while begging her to be great?
Our hands are up, Sir.

No sir, yes Sir,
America is not at her best, Sir.
Why must we apologize
For our size,
For our desire to rise
Off our knees?
Must we ask for permission
To be on a mission
For change?
Doesn't it seem strange
That we are wrong when we walk,
Wrong when we balk,
Wrong when we kneel
Or explain how we feel
Because you don't share our experiences, our pain, Sir?

No, Sir, No Sir.
You are not right, Sir.
You are misinformed, Sir.
We do not mean harm, Sir.
Although you cover our issue in mud.
We do not ask permission
To be on a mission
To uncover our truth.
We need no permission
To take a stand.
Yes, we love our country, Sir.
Even when She is broken, Sir.
Love means fixing what's wrong, Sir.

Yes, our hands are where you can see, Sir.
No tricks up our sleeves, Sir.
We just want you to see, Sir,
The treatment, the injustice, Sir.
Yes, it's better than it was before, Sir.
But She can be better if we uncover her sores, Sir.
We are mothers, fathers,
Concerned citizens, veterans, soldiers too…Sir Listen, …wait…it is true…we can prove it…
Our hands ARE up, Sir. We ARE on our knees, Sir.
Stop! DON'T SHOOT! Sir.

Freedom to Live, People

Ty (When the protesters in the street were White)

I just can't
with my screen!
All the misinformation
people believe.
The angry voices
and what they mean,
about people.

I'm sick of seeing
the American flag
brandished for medical
advice that's bad.
Because people love
the life they had,
more than people.

I'm tired of hearing
that caution is fear.
As if science
is what cowardice hears.
You think a mask
makes freedom disappear?
Choosing ME over "We the people."

Newsflash my friends
of political memes:
Your freedoms of life,
liberty, and ease
are preserved by laws
and *responsibilities*
that protect ALL people.

This is not the land
of loudest defiance,
where the healthy scream,
"Fuck the weak!" with riots.
I don't give a shit if you've
missed pubs and stylists.
I give a shit about people.

Why don't you?

Freedom to Live, People

Ty (When the protesters in the street were Black)

Well I don't know
Anymore,
Nothing can surprise,
I can't ignore,
The crazy shit
That I abhor
About people.

You don't love neighbor,
You don't love God.
It's all a fucking,
Disgusting façade.
You'll march for privilege,
But not for love
Of *my* people.

Roles Reversed

Imani

If the roles were reversed,
How'd you feel to be guilty first?
How would you feel if you grew up
Fearing the red and blue lights that pull up
behind you?
Would you know to
Drive somewhere well lit and safe,
Or how your hands should be placed?
Would fear or anger settle in your spine,
Knowing that you crossed no line?
Would a baton breaching the skin
Remind you of the skin you're in?
Or your body feel the same pain,
When your face is pressed against concrete and blood-stained?
If the roles were reversed, would you simply lay there
and accept your plight?
Or would you demand your rights,
Knowing that you could be the next
Killed by someone sworn to protect.
Would blue lives matter then?
Or the skin you're in?
If the roles were reversed,
How'd you feel to be guilty first?

Dark Days

Kate

Will says we'll pay the bills.
The mortgage we'll make,
And if the kids take a break
From soccer and swim,
Maybe that's a win,
All in bed by eight again.

Shawna says don't worry it's fine.
Jack left her with a cushion.
Savings, she's not afraid to use 'em.
The restaurant will open up soon,
Back up and running by end of June.
How can she know? What will we do?

Imani says to remember my faith.
Trust that God is not surprised,
Don't let this moment pass me by.
Take this time to use my voice,
Cry out for justice in this noise.
Hold tight my family, for them rejoice.

Will says we'll pay the bills.
Shawna says don't worry it's fine.
Imani says to remember my faith…
While hate and sickness take their kills,
Filling our city, hearts and minds.
Who can find hope in these dark days?

I Ain't Looking for Trouble

Darius

I ain't looking for Trouble.
Trouble's looking for me.
Especially when my big Blackness
Is the first thing you see.
When my color replaces my humanity.
When a preconception tried and found me guilty.
When I raised my hands and said, "Don't shoot me."
When I bent a knee and asked you to see
The injustice all around me.
All the Black men in my community
Ain't a threat. I plea
That you release
All the negative energy
That clouds your judgement. Free
Your mind and free me.
Nah, I ain't looking for Trouble,
But Trouble finds me.

Marching

Aliyah (Haikus)

Protest signs in hand,
Vibrant energy abounds,
Crowd surges forward.

Heart and feet pounding,
Sweat and tears soak through my mask,
Chanting every name.

Protest signs in hand,
The air charged with hope and fear.
Police stand close by.

Heart and feet pounding.
The pavement feels our anguish.
Black and bright we march.

Brothers

Sisters

Brothers…
I have so many.
Bold and bashful,
Bearded and bare-faced,
Bald and loc'd,
Big and beautiful.
Black.

Brothers…
I have so many.
Gainfully employed, unemployed, self-employed.
Hardworking and easy going,
Locked up and lifted up,
Lit as fuck.
Black.

Brothers…
I have so many.
Pray for so many.
Worry for so many.
Shake my head at so many.
Love so many.
Black.

Brothers…
I have so many.
I pray that a knee never touches their neck,
That they give and receive respect—equally.
That they stand on their feet,
Kneel for their beliefs,
And are loved and not feared
For the color of their skin.
Black.

Nobody's Martyr

Brothers

Man, I don't want to be
Nobody's martyr.
I ain't wake up today
Planning on doing anything
But survive,
Eat, and feed my family.

Man, I ain't
Nobody's martyr.
I've done some shit,
And been through some shit
That would topple the strongest man.
But I don't deserve to die.

Man, I can't be
Nobody's martyr.
My feet are rooted in my neighborhood, future, and past deeds.
I'm triggered by what y'all think of me.
Always Black before I'm a man.
Always guilty before human.

Man, I ain't
Nobody's martyr.
I'm a man
Weighted with history and your bigotry.
I'm a man
Before I open my mouth,
Before you get a chance to see
That I'm better than on my worst day,
Even when I made choices that
Fed me for a day but
Locked me up and
Lost me the right to vote.

Man, I ain't wanna be
Nobody's martyr.
Didn't ask for it, not built for it.
Can barely fight for myself

With my head down
Or my hands out,
Vote suppressed,
And taxed without representation
Although my transgression,
Paid for
But unforgiven.
Judged on every application,
Home and job.
Nah, I ain't looking for pity,
Just let me be.
I ain't nobody's martyr,
And I ain't trying to be.

Kindling

About Kindling

Although a single match lit fires all over America on May 25, 2020, the kindling for those fires was already there. The mamas had already wept. The sons and daughters had already left this world, murdered by ignorance and hate. Their Black bodies had already been laid down with prayers that their sacrifice might at least become the kindling of change.

No one who had seen this kind of pain, who had hurt this kind of hurt, could escape falling deep into memory when that single match lit up the night. The kindling that sparked was their pain. The kindling that caught fire and burned had a name and names, had a dream and dreams, had a future…stolen and buried.

This section, *Kindling*, gives voice to those memories, past *and* present.

Where Is My Boy

Mama

Where is my boy?
Should've been home by now.
Probably has him a crowd.
Never seen so much joy.
He'll come home telling stories.
I can never stay mad.
So animated, we'll both laugh,
to hear him tell of his glories.
But wait—is it really 10:30?
That boy knows to be here,
knows how I get when my fear
has me pacing and worried.
I think I'll try him again.
Baby, pick up the phone.
Son, I need you at home.
Tomorrow, you can see your friends.
Jack's said Son left at nine.
Oh, thank God! I hear a car.
No.....no, Son would never knock…
"Good evening, ma'am. Tonight…"
"No…"
"You're Son's Mama, is that right?"
"Ma'am?
Tonight, there was an altercation…
An unfortunate situation…
Ma'am, can you stand?
Ma'am?"
"No! God!
Where is my boy?"

Gone

Kate	Will

Tell me he's not

                    gone.

Tell me he's home.

                    Gone.

Tell me his future's,

                    gone,

as wide as it's long.

                    Gone.

Tell me you're wrong!

                    Gone.

No. Will, he can't be

                    gone.

Dammit, he's not!

                    Gone.

Stop saying he's

                    gone.

Stop!

But I saw him today!

                    Gone.

Biggest smile on his face!

                    Gone.

Friday he's got a game,

                    gone,

and Saturday a date.

                    Gone.

Sweet girl, pretty face,

                    gone,

I think Charisse is her name.

                    Gone.

Comes to Jack's to see Son,

                    gone,

been eyeing him for months.

                    Gone.

No, baby he's got dreams—

                    gone.

(Kate)	(Will)
Like his Mama, big belief!	
	Gone.
Oh God, Mama!	
	Gone.
Will, *who's with Mama*?	
	Gone.
I don't understand…	
	gone.
Son's got so many plans,	
	gone.
Will, no…not Son…	
	gone.
In a million, he's one!	
	Gone.
He just can't really be	
	gone.
Will, baby, look at me.	
	Gone.
Were you there in the street?	
	Gone.
Did you see him……*bleed*?	
	Gone.
Shhh, no more. Don't speak.	
	Gone!
Baby, shhh. Don't speak.	

Tears on the Rim

Mama

Have you ever been numb?
Where the time passes
And you don't know how?
Where you couldn't cry tears
But your soul walked in circles
Looking for an outlet for the pain?

      Then they came.

Those endless tears that neither
Heal, console, or wash the sadness away.
Salty and sad,
They question, "Why?"
Even when the answer can't erase the pain.
The loss too new, too dear, too raw
To process with anything but more
Tears.

Every minute
They hover on the edge of disbelief
And acknowledgment.
Walking on the edge and balancing
On the rim of a glass overfilled
Waiting to spill.
Then, relentless in their journey,
They travel
Along the planes of a face filled with grief for
The loss too new, too dear, too raw
For anything but more
Tears.

      They don't stop.

Maybe for a minute…
As if to collect themselves.
Then a memory, a smell, silence, or a hug
Welcomes their return.
This time they arrive with
Unbelievable grief,
Or anger,
Or a smile.
Unpredictable is their presence
And purpose.
Yet today, they are welcomed.
They usher you into heaven
As loved ones open their arms to greet you.
Even when your absence from me is
Too dear, too new, too raw
For anything more than
Tears.

We're Never Fast Enough

Aliyah

There's an ache,
an empty hollowing.
It chisels and scrapes,
and I can't escape.
Instead, in death,
my soul's following.
Down to Son's grave,
6 feet and deeper
it's calling.
Digging and digging,
hopelessness gnawing.
Unearthing what's buried,
in grief again falling.
His face
In my dreams,
my name
he's still hollerin'.
But I can't run fast enough.
We're never fast enough.

Praise the Lord

Shawna, Imani (The Sunday after Son's death, Imani and Shawna sit beside one another at church.)

Shawna: Praise the Lord—

Imani: I'm strugglin' with those words.

Shawna: Every promise, I've ever heard

Both: feels like a lie.

Shawna: And I can't cry,

Imani: like this,

Shawna: not in front of my kids,

Imani: but there's sickness in our souls
                and waiting outside.

Shawna: How I've tried

Both: to pray,

Imani: to find honest words to say,

Shawna: but I can't escape, the way it feels
                when goodness dies.

Both: Praise the Lord…?
                I'm strugglin' with those words!
                Every promise, I've ever heard
                feels like a lie…
                Lord, tell me why?

My Son

Mama

Sitting here thinking about my boy,
My son.
Can't stop the salty tears or curb the grief,
Of losing
My son.
People sending condolences and well wishes for
My son.
Can't erase this ache in my heart,
I'm missing
My son.
Asking what made them take him so soon,
My son.
Pushing down anger, trying to find forgiveness for those
Who took
My son.
Holding on to my Bible, my faith, and praying for
My son.
It's so silent in this house,
Without the laughter of
My son.
Holding on to the belief that I will see him again,
My son.
Tears, they don't soothe this overwhelming ache in my heart.

I love him,

My son.

Tainted With Sadness

Brothers

How can I help,
When I'm covered in grief
And anger?
How can I lift my head,
When the burden of knowledge
Of wrongdoing sits on my shoulders
And I want to fight, to cry out
And to scream, "IT'S ENOUGH!"
When I mean, "It's too much."
How can I keep forgiving
Your refusal to see me as human,
Whole, made in the image of God,
Worthy of life?
How can I live in perfect peace
Alongside you
When you fear the color of my skin,
The size of my body,
Hate the kink of my hair,
The intelligence behind my eyes,
The sound of my voice
When I call out injustice, hypocrisy,
And inequity in your actions?
How can we coexist,
When you use your privilege
As an opportunity to halt my existence?

I don't know…

But I'm tired of having to prove
My worth
And "yes sir" you until my shoulders
Are slumped with the indignity
Of your expectations.
My eyes are tainted with sadness
For the loss of my brothers,
Fathers, sons, and daughters
From your eagerness to take a life
You long suspected was not worth

Your brothers', fathers', sons', and daughters' lives.
I'm angry with the conversations
That don't start until something happens to
Shine a spotlight on
Your type of justice.
I'm pissed off that I must protest,
Kneel, shout, cry, and videotape
Twisted actions to prove to the world
That we are not the "land of the free" or "innocent until proven guilty."

And you...
You turn off the news that shows the pain I feel.
You say, "He must have done something" or "why couldn't he just..."
As if the burden of proof of my humanity is
On me
As I lay on the ground with my
hands up,
Follow your instructions
to stop,
Sit in my living room,
And jog in my neighborhood.
You don't want to see me.
You don't want to hear the tears my family cries.
Or the anger of a community long past the excuses
Of a system not made to protect us,
Or sanctify our rights in this land.
You don't see how we are
Tainted with sadness.
That we are still fighting a battle
Long fought for since
Our feet touched the shores.

Old News

Sisters

This ain't new.
This death ain't new.
We ain't surprised by the
Lost breath or voice straining,
"I can't breathe."
The blood soaking into the concrete
Has soaked the soil
For hundreds of years.
Blacks been wailing and mourning
Our fathers and brothers
Taken by the hand of hatred
Justified by past failings,
Prejudices, and pride.
No, this death ain't new.

This pain ain't new.
We been wounded for generations
As women cried
And shielded their babies from
Viewing daddy hanging in a tree,
Shot in a car,
Drug down the street,
Laying on the ground
Underneath a foot or two,
Handcuffed, bound, bloody—
Still.
No, this sight ain't new.

This weariness ain't new.
Tired of Black meaning
Death before proof
And guilty before human.
Been worn down by the burden
Of forgiveness
For acts God didn't sanction,
But we've been used to
All too often.
Forgiveness we can't earn,

Buy, or borrow.
The cost of Blackness
Much too high.
Forgiveness we've been trained to offer up like prayers
For a promised land Moses and Martin saw,
But we've yet to encounter.
No, this burden ain't new.

Black anger ain't new.
Contained, yet often
Close to the surface,
Hidden behind a face
Trained in the art of concealment.
Brown eyes clouded by memories
And promises of equality
And inclusion
That missed the mark
From the first signature
On a Constitution
Covered in Black ink.
Rage bubbling through
The pores of skin
Darkened
By God,
Envied because of its beauty,
Yet feared for its strength.
No, this rage ain't new.

These fires ain't new.
Ignited by years of oversight.
Black blood, pain, weariness,
and anger fanned the flames.
Judgment showed up
To condemn the reaction
To the wrong repeatedly forgiven.
Yet, the kindling was ignored.
Just a frozen image on the screen,
The lens caught democracy slacking,
Again.

This death ain't new.
This pain ain't new.
This burden ain't new.
This anger ain't new.
This rage ain't new.

These fires ain't new.

Culture on Your Shoulders

Shawna

Hold your head up high
And be better than me.
Always try your best.
Let your intelligence lead.
You've got to be 100 times smarter
And work 100 times harder
For them to give you credit.
Culture on your shoulders, now don't you forget it.

Let me know when you leave,
Where you're going, and take your ID.
Go straight there, let me know when you arrive.
I need to know you're safe, know you're alive.
You know I can't sleep when you're not home.
I worry when you're out all alone.
Now repeat after me.
Culture on your shoulders, this you better believe.

This march you're going to,
Make sure to represent what's true.
Don't get caught in rioting and violence.
Don't stray from your group and respect the police.
They are there to protect and serve without pause.
But some of them, the few of them, will beat you without cause.
Focus on the movement, be careful in the crowd.
Culture on your shoulders, now go, make me proud.

For Mama. For Him.

Will

Mama came by the restaurant today.
We're still not re-opened. Covid delays.
Some customers hate us for it.
Some customers love us for being safe.
I'm too burdened to know what's right.
But I opened the door for Mama.

I will always open the door for Mama.
Be damned the sign in the window that states,
"For the safety of our customers and employees
Jack's dining room is closed to the public, but we
have curbside take-out now available."
But Mama isn't public. She's family.

Because Son was one of ours.
Because I trained him. Because I loved him.
We all did. Incredible kid. A light in this darkness.
I will always see his eyes in her eyes.
Big, brown, little flecks of amber.
Feel that constriction in my chest. Remember.

Because seeing Mama makes me relive his death again.
When I see her at the door, I hear the sirens.
When I hear the sirens, I hear Aliyah's screams.
When I hear the screams, I'm trapped like in a dream.
His body's back in the street. Aliyah's sobbing there at his feet.
And Mama's home waiting for a boy who won't come back.

Until he comes back to me, when I see Mama.
Through the glass, now in her mask,
it covers the smiles she forces.
I see pained eyes I know still cry each morning.
Like a wave, my rage comes back then, takes me under.
No, he wasn't armed, wouldn't harm, he was the best kid!

So, I open the door for Mama.
I get her anything she wants. And I can feel him in the kitchen.
She tries to make the moment less awkward, and I hate myself again.
Because she tries to ease my pain, to bear mine and hers
in these impossible, hellish days, but all that I can say
is, "Mama, please, come again." For him.

RUN

Kate[3]

We run.
> To remember others who can't.
>> To make way for tomorrow's runners.
>>> To feel—*something like hope.*
>>>> To resist hate *and* complacency.
>>>>> To expose the lie of liberty.
>>>>>> To proclaim we're not as we should be.
>>>>>>> ***TO CONDEMN WHITE SUPREMACY*!**
>>>>>> To display what it means to live free.
>>>>> To rewrite rewritten history.
>>>>> To lend sympathy and solidarity.
>>>> To feel—*something like hope.*
>>> To make way for tomorrow's runners.
>> To remember others who can't.

We run.

---

[3] Kate wrote this for Ahmaud Arbury. She wrote it for Son and so many sons and daughters. She wrote this when she ran on May 8, 2020, Ahmaud's 26th birthday. She wrote this when her kids ran with her, 2.23 miles in his honor because Ahmaud was killed on 2-23-2020. Kate wrote this when her daughter chanted, "No more hate!" all over the neighborhood as they ran. She wrote this when it mattered to DO SOMETHING. To MOVE. To do ANYTHING at all. It still matters.

The Lost Ones Knew

Imani

I closed my eyes
And took a breath.
My lungs filled
And chills tickled my skin.
Just a breath
And all that was good flowed in.
Whoever would've thought something so simple
Would feel so good.

　　Then I thought…

The lost ones knew.
All of the men and women
Dead on a street with a knee
To their throat
Crushed under the weight
Of fear and bias
Built on keeping one group "safe"
And another contained.

The lost ones who never sought
To be kindling
For the flames of injustice
Which rise up and engulf
The walls of brutality.
Those who just wanted to breathe.

I closed my eyes
and took a breath.
Just a breath.
A breath for the lost ones.
Those who
Begged for, fought for,
Kneeled for, longed for
Blind justice, colorless justice.

The lost ones knew
How good it felt to breathe.

They knew the plight of a people
Who whispered and yelled,
"You don't have to
Make room for me
In your world.
I just need enough to
Breathe."

Son

Imani (for Mama, *MSG*, Ps. 9.11-13, 18-20)[4]

"Sing your songs to
Zion-dwelling God,
tell his stories to
everyone you meet:
How he tracks down
killers yet keeps
his eye on us,
registers every
whimper and moan.
Be kind to me, God;
I've been kicked
around long enough.
...No longer will the
poor be nameless—
no more humiliation
for the humble. Up, God!
Aren't you fed up
...Shake them up, God!"

Ps. 9:11-13, 18-20

[4] Peterson, Eugene H. *The Message.* Colorado Springs, CO: NavPress, 2002. Print.

Burning

Just a Pinch

Nancy's Blood (The silent lessons Nancy's blood taught her, passed down for generations.)[5]

Recipe for Maintenance of Whiteness as Righteous Status Quo
(*make and repeat as often as needed*)

Ingredients:

Just a pinch of Blackness
(*to affirm your own goodness*)
1 ½ cups of rightness
(*like yeast they must see you rise*)
3 tbsp of comfort
(*You shall not be needlessly made to suffer*)
1 sack of history
(*unfortunately, this can't be left out*)
2 cups of holy water
(*there's no better fallback than faith*)
All dreams of revolution
(*keep separate from other ingredients, lest they become too hard to extract*)
Rounded tsp of privilege
(*never leave this out*)

Directions:

No need to preheat the flames. Your status, your power has always burned bright.
First, grease the pan with privilege. Your effort should not cost a crumb of you.
Next, crush dreams to powder. Then set these aside.
Dilute the whole sack of history. Use holy water. Nothing is more effective.
Mix all remaining ingredients into diluted history. Be sure to leave out crushed dreams. Rightness will dominate the batter when mixed sufficiently.
Pour into privilege greased pan and bake in flames. Let burn. Let blacken. Don't scrape off the char.
Remove and serve hot. On top of crushed dreams.
Don't serve yourself.
Repeat whenever new dreams take shape. This recipe is tried and true.
It has never failed.

---

[5] Nancy did not write these words. She does not realize they are tucked into the folds of her life. But they are. She has lived them. She has even used them, whether or not she saw it then.

400 Years

Imani

400 years
Israel was enslaved in Egypt.

400 years
You were silent, your people exiled from your rule, oppressed by pagan kings.

400 years
Black bodies were enslaved in America, then falsely freed, then still not free.

400 years
And they still don't see, still don't believe.

400 years
Lord, it's been too long.

I'm Running Outta Room

Shawna (Early June)

I'm running outta room
For names in the afro on my T-shirt.
Is it a privilege
for their Black names
To be scrolled in white
As the tears roll down faces,
With fists held high,
With voices raised,
And the
City burning?
Should I have to print
"I can't breathe"
In a special font
That denotes
I'm not your enemy?
No.
Not today or any day.

I'm running outta room
On my timeline.
Can't keep scrolling through the names and faces
Of a brother, sister, father, son
Who took their last breath
As their last breath was taken
By the badge and the shield,
And a system
Who sees
Us as
The enemy
Today
And 400 years of days.

I'm running outta room
In my patience
To explain
Yet again,
Why the signs are waving,
Voices are raised,
Feet are marching,
Fires are burning,
T-shirts are made
With all the names
That don't fit...
In the afro
On my T-shirt
Today.

Can't Sleep

Aliyah

Darius is enraged.
Tossing in my bed sheets,
Can't sleep.
Eyes fixed on our screens,
Can't breathe
Or grieve
Or even believe
Anyone is really listening.

I hear what he's sayin'.
I see what he sees,
Can't sleep.
Eyes fixed on our screens,
Can't breathe
Drowning in grief
For Son, and sons. I'm already bereaved
And no one ever listening.

So in battle, we're engaged.
Protesting in these streets.
Can you sleep?
Eyes fixed on your screens,
Is it easy to breathe
When we're shouting, lamenting our grief,
Begging you, this city, this country to see?
But are you? Is anyone listening?

D and me, from hope we're estranged.
Tossing in my bed sheets,
Can't sleep.
Eyes fixed on our screens,
Can't breathe
Needing salvation from such grief!
Needing to see change in you to believe
That what we're fighting for
        will ever be more
                than just a dream.

It's All Wrong

Nancy

Now Jan's boy, Will, is at it.
Posting "Black Lives Matter."
As if his mother didn't take him to church,
With my Michael, with Gretchen.
He should know better.
Jesus loves ALL.

And hasn't he seen it?
The drugs, the gangs,
the pants that hang.
The welfare abused,
His inheritance taken,
His daddy taxed and taxed,
Their needs relentless.

All so they can take his job!
Jan told me about it.
Her boy was more qualified, been there longer,
But some Black woman took it.
Took the weekday shift he wanted.
He had earned it. Not her.
Wanted more time with Kate and the kids.
But his boss let that girl stroll in and have it.
For the numbers. For the image.

And for what?
So now his mother can be called a racist?
So now he can be labeled privileged?
So now they can destroy our country
out in the streets?
Thieving and burning.
More dangerous than ever.

They're just angry
that they haven't worked as hard as he has.
That they can't get their lives together.
Can't stay out of jail,
Can't make something of themselves without his help,

Without his sacrifice.
No other people act like this!
Yet somehow, now, they've got him angry too!

I don't understand.
I can't.
What is happening to the world?
What is happening to everyone?
To America—
        the America I know and love?

But I tell you,
I wouldn't eat there now if they were open,
and I've been going there for years!
Dining room closed for safety?
With the employees they have in there?
Aliyah? I think that's her name.
And that boy Darius she lives with, too?
They've never been unkind,
but this rioting is insane.
And I hear they're marching.
Doing God knows what to this city.
No, that place has never been safe.
Only now I see it.

Outside the Church Doors

Kate

My enemies,
    who were not my enemies,
fellow believers who spew venom and hate.
It poisons them,
    And it poisons me.

I try to spit their hatred out
    of my mouth!
    Of my soul!
Without spewing more,
without excusing wrongs with silence.

I find myself
    reaching
    for anything
that is more,
    for anything
that is good.
But alas, their venom still spreads
    a coat so thick,
    it covers all I see.

If I could with light,
    with holy fire,
    I would burn
it all
to the ground.

I would light up the dross,
    the impurity that adulterates a nation's soul,
    and I would skim, no, I would *dredge*, it off,
with force and with fury.

All their professions of hate and exemplarism!
All their pride that declares
they alone have the right
    to live and define liberty;
they alone have the right

to rule and shape the rules;
they alone have the right
    to walk—freely—in a darkness
        they have come to call the light.

It is not their right!
It is not right!
It is not!
But it is,
    how it is,
and it is poison.

Still, I see the shackles—
    when pride and self become their gods.
    when they believe the lies that ignore their flaws.
    when they claim to love and trust you, God,
    but they do not love your people.

When they clothe themselves in ungodly weapons.
    Guns, and flags, and words like knives!
        Racism and hate like bile,
        fists and knees that choke out life!
    They strip themselves of masks that love!
        Simple acts, so easily done.
        They throw off sacrifice for fun,
    but they do not love your people.

They cling to the way things were,
    when the poor still hungered,
    and the marginalized still thirsted.
    When the minority still perished
        at the hand of their kin,
        yet they cannot see their sin?
        God! They cannot see their sin!

My enemies,
    who were not my enemies,
Stop! Stop spewing your venom and hate!
Stop poisoning you!
    Stop poisoning me!
    Stop poisoning every, single thing!

God help us.

Come, swift and full of flame, Lord;
  come shine your light
in this darkness that overwhelms me,
a darkness that covers everything.

I cannot see.
  God!
I cannot see.
I need your light.

Sinners

Ty

We're turning over tables,
where you fattened up your house.
You think we're sinners who are wayward?
We see you living high like Faust.
Why would we loot, and burn, and pillage?
Your shrines to comfort and status destroy?
We've never lived White in your village,
and we will no longer be your boy.

Leftist Lies

J.R.

Flaming Liberals with their matches,
trying to burn the America I love.
Can't stand to stop their blaming tactics,
despite the lies it's all built on.
Race and riot is not our problem;
masks won't protect us from their flames.
They think they're righteous, but God is sovereign.
I bet they don't even know his name.

Using God's Name

Imani

What does God say?
When he hears his name?
Wave after wave after wave
of hot anger,
so shallow in grace.
Ears that hear what they want,
deaf to truths God has taught.
When will the first be last
and the last first?
Our thirst isn't wrong.
And our song's not just fire—
it's tears and brokenness,
we're tired.
It's the Psalms, and it's pain.
Yes, when God hears his name,
What does God say?

Even the Saints

Brothers

You can't support the cause
Because
It was I who died.
You have no pride
And no sympathy
For my family.
Just paint me as a criminal
Your value for my life—minimal.
Full of sin like us all.
Let he who's done no wrong fall.
Would it then be wrong for a life to end?
Or right for protests to begin?
Even the saints have sinned.

You can't see your wrongness,
Only my Blackness.
Can't support freedom for me
Because you fail to see
My humanity
Or that equality and equity
Are practiced differently when I appear.
When I say "justice," "victim" is what you hear.
You fail to see mistreatment,
Yet call my pleas entitlement.
Wrapped up in your rightness, you doubt
The evidence until I shout.
Then tell me to be quiet.
Call my protest a riot.
Call my pain to question, again and again.
While my eyes turn to heaven asking "When?"
Even the saints have sinned.

Oh, you saints…
You saints who call on
African Angels
To intervene on your behalf.
Speaking in unknown tongues as we gasp
At the audacity of your arrogance,

Your ignorance,
And holier than thou-ness
As you call on *OUR* African ancestors,
Those you denied us long ago,
To lift your shallow satan above what's right,
Above our sons and daughters.
How sinful, Saint!
Using our faithfulness
To shackle us!
To bind us
And misguide us.
We know now what we knew then,
Even the saints have sin.

Privilege

Imani

One bird
perches on the fence, on the roof, on the yard.
One bird
wakes in the shadow, in the rain, in the dark.

With wings
one flitters here, over there, all around.
With wings
one sings of flight, sings of sight, from the ground.

"But we're both birds?"
sings the bird, hatched in safety, up in his nest.
"But we're both birds?"
laments the bird, whose worn out wings still garner less.

How will both fly?
One falls to flight, the other jumps, only to stand.
How will both fly?
If stolen sky is not returned, to the bird on the land?

My Shoes

Brothers

We can't have

the same

perspective.

You've never been

in my shoes,

never seen my views.

Love One Another

Will

"But the greatest commandment," said mother,
"is love your God and love one another."
So, I'm trying, showing commitment to my brothers,
yet suddenly I'm the foreign, the mistaken, the "other."

Gretchen

Michael says our parents' generation won't get it.
There's too much to lose if wrongdoing's admitted.
Yet he's not yet sure what wrongdoing's been committed.
While I fear discovering all that has been acquitted.

Nancy

What is happening to my Michael's generation?
Why are they even questioning the need for reparations?
Yes, slavery was bad, and of course discrimination,
but the way they were raised is not some racist aberration!

Will

Some days I want to shake them and scream, "Wake up!
You've been misled and misleading about love.
Do you really think that all you have was fairly won?
Do you really think all this is cool with God's son?"

Gretchen

The marginalized have pushed out of the margins.
Their outcry isn't making space for White pardons.
I didn't know, but on my ignorance, they've barged in.
If it's all true, why have our hearts become so hardened?

Nancy

We're not rich, but we're comfortable; we've worked hard.
Should I feel shame for being disciplined, for being smart?
No one is saying that racism isn't wrong!
But why can't we just love one another and move on?

Over

J.R.

History is history.
Behind us.
Gone and done.
Over.
Why we gotta dredge it all up again?

I know it's dirt.
Our history.
Dark. Ugly. And soaked in blood.
We all know that!
But American soil ain't just bloody dirt no more!

Sure, we grew cotton,
But we grew dreams, too.
Watered with clean water,
grown in good soil.

We also grew opportunity,
and even freedom!
And we ain't put no damn fence around it
(Even if now we need a wall so America can feed itself).
But all we grew,
every beautiful stalk of freedom,
every bloomin' opportunity
was crops for the takin'.
For everyone born here.
For ALL real Americans!

No one here now is a slave to anyone.
Not today.
If you pick cotton, you get paid.
Honest work, for honest Americans.
But these fires ain't honest.
They have one goal alone.
It's a reckoning, alright,
But not the revolutionary kind
This is just hate. Power.
Flame and fury.

And it's gonna burn this country to the ground.
It's not gonna avenge no slaves.
It ain't gonna equalize something that's already equal.
It's just gonna leave us all blackened.

Black and bruised.
Black and burned.

But it too will become history.
And history is history.
Behind us.
Gone and done.
Over.
I'm ready for that.

Our Fight

Will　　　　　　　　　　　**Silent Right**

There are a few who engage.
Most of those,
they rage,
but their majority
hasn't come, to this fight.

　　　　　　　　　　　　　　It's not our fight,

　　　　　　they say,

　　　　　　　　　　　　　　Not our price to pay.
　　　　　　　　　　　　　　It's not our burden to weigh
　　　　　　　　　　　　　　or lose sleep at night.

So, they go on
with their days.
Busy with work and soccer games.
Nine to five and Saturday,
everything's alright.

　　　　　　　　　　　　　　Sure, we're White,
　　　　　　　　　　　　　　but that's okay.
　　　　　　　　　　　　　　We've never, ever owned a slave.
　　　　　　　　　　　　　　Honest believers, who always pray
　　　　　　　　　　　　　　for our brothers' plight.

　　　　　　　　　　　　　　It's just out of sight.
　　　　　　　　　　　　　　It's not ours,
　　　　　　　　　　　　　　not mine,
　　　　　　　　　　　　　　　　　you see?
　　　　　　　　　　　　　　It's not our fight.

Not It, Not I

Silent Right

What dog in the fight have I?
None of this is in my world. I deny
That race ever crosses my mind.
My family, my friends, we're colorblind.
I'm surprised by the violence I've seen on the TV.
But it's not in my life, not in my community.
We have friends, Black friends, who mean so much to us.
They've never mentioned racism and all the other fuss.
They know we don't see color; we are all the same.
We don't need to discuss hashtags, marches, and names.
I mean, we don't talk about it. Why would we?
It doesn't affect or include me.
This isn't my fight and doesn't touch my life.
Racism, protests, and unrest aren't mine.
I'd rather not give attention to anything that divides our nation.
I don't need to join in the conversation.
I have nothing to do with and nothing to say,
About what's going on in the streets today.
I have no monstrous intentions to spy.
I'm not racist so this isn't my fight.
This isn't my struggle…
Not me, not it, not I.

Silent Privilege

Shawna

Inequity screams at you from screens,
And in your ivory isolation, you claim it's unseen,
Unheard, unknown, and un-yours...really?
Does your duty to America stop when we want equality?
Do you not shake the hand of inequity as you turn away
From faces, those unseen faces, whose color you "don't see?"
Playing "Not It" with racism and whispering "not me."
Your silent privilege shows up when you don't speak out,
Speak up or listen to the shouts.
You claim immunity to the pain in America, the land of the free.
Yet you proudly speak of the "Black friend" you invite for coffee.
That one friend you are happy to see.
Well maybe...just maybe
You should ask them about the silent privilege you wield.
Your superpower, held up like a shield.
Privilege visibly clouding your vision of the vices
Streaming through our electronic devices.
Ask them, the token you've claimed to cherish and hold dear,
Ask them about the uncertainty and fear
They experience knowing their skin bears witness
To the politics of hate and divisiveness.
Would they allow you into their Blackness?
Would you visit their experiences? And could they confess
The pain of being declared dangerous by those sworn to serve and protect?
Colorless in their blue pact
Against Blackness.
Would your "Black friend" invite you to protest?
Would you participate in the call for justice?
Or would you, head turned, eyes cast away
Have the silent privilege and nerve to say,
"Not I, not it, not me."
Watch out! Inaction, unspoken words, and your absence are in fact the emblem
Declaring your apathy
And your Silent privilege.

What We Have in Common

Will

We all want to be free.
We just don't agree
on what that means.
Most of us are tired of the divisiveness.
We want better to be out there,
hope to be real,
unity to be more than a dream.
And I could say
to focus on this,
on what makes us the same—
to take a moment to see
past the battle lines,
to take the small peace we can find,
no matter how thin
how fleeting,
to take what we can get.
But I won't.

Because we also want to be brave.

Who has ever kept their freedom without courage?
Who has ever slept at night,
at peace with themselves,
by hiding in the safety of shadows?
Not I.
Not now.
Especially not now.
Freedom is costly.
Ideals take maintenance,
thoughtfulness,
raised voices
hard choices,
but surprisingly
this choice is not hard.

To say what I believe,
To let passionate conviction
escape the boundary of my lips—

to let that boundary fall away
just feels right.
I too need my sleep at night.
So…
I believe in the equality
and the dignity of all people.
And I believe
that what we are now
is not enough.

This Is My Life

Darius   **Silent Right**

This is humanity's fight.
This isn't Black, this isn't White.
This isn't sit back as long as you're nice.
This is my life.

                                    {Silence…

                                                    …}

This isn't a spectator's sport.
This isn't forgiven by honest, hard work.
This isn't just fixed by prayers to the Lord.
This is my hurt.

                                    {Silence…

                                                    …}

This isn't absolved by your Sunday service.
This isn't resolved because a handful have heard us.
This isn't exemption because you're nervous.

                                    But it doesn't concern us.

That's how you hurt us.

This is my life.

"I Am"

Imani

They say,
> "You are not."

He says,
> "I am."

They say,
> "You are not able
>> to live by the rules."
>> to garner what's mine."
>> to conquer the Dream."
>> to see how I'm blind."

They say,
> "You are not."

He says,
> "I am."

If

Shawna

If you listen to my voice,
           you might hear your own.

                                             Mama

                            If a mother's tears could heal,
                    the world would be well.

Aliyah

If I seem angry, ask me why.
           When I tell you, *hear me*.

I Don't Know What to Say

Gretchen

I don't know what to say.
I don't know what to pray.
But if we fight today,
fire will light the way.

So, I need to find the words,
though the truth may burn.
My racism overturn;
my complacency unlearn.

Because I don't know what to say!
I don't know what to pray!
But not knowing is not okay.
That's my hate just hidden away.

So, I need to find the words,
join hands with those I've hurt.
Beg forgiveness I haven't earned;
show repentance for cries unheard.

If You Ask Me

Imani

If you ask me,
I'll tell you about all the ones before me.
Their stories drift in the wind
And sometimes settle in the
Retelling of stories soaked in the tears of families
Missing the flowers, and even the weeds too soon
Yanked from their garden.
Stories etched on the faces and hearts of a people trying to
Forgive and forge on.
Stories that define a family, community, and a country.
But would you listen?

If you ask me,
I'll tell you about the names
In the recesses of a hashtag or
On a t-shirt stained with some long-forgotten meal.
I'll recount the cause abandoned by those claiming piety to justice and equality.
I'll highlight a movement abandoned because the banner—Black Lives Matter—
Didn't include blue.
About Justice denied by experiences denied,
Even those captured in the truth of a lens.
Of outcries heard, disbelief stirred,
Marches organized then…forgotten.
At least until the next news cycle.
And, if you ask me,
I'll tell you there will always be a next.
But would you listen?

If you ask me,
I'll tell you about the conflict of those like me.
Born under the ambiguity of greatness, expectation, faith, and doubt.
A slave to the duplicity of a country and community
That beseeches us to "Be American,"
Fight American,
Pledge American,
While stapling a descriptor onto our identities…
"African…American,"
And sorts us, White from yolk.

If you ask me, I'll tell you we are both and neither.
But would you listen?

If you ask me,
I'll try to explain
In words you can embrace,
Unlike my color which you choose
To sometimes see,
Condemn,
Praise,
Or pretend to not see
To prove your liberality.
I'll try to describe our collective hesitation
At sharing our truths
About our experiences,
For we know you can never truly know,
Even when you march, kneel, bleed, or lay beside us.
I will tell you that we have cursed you,
Yet still forgive crimes against us and pray fervently—
While waiting for justice,
Hopeful for your enlightenment
Yet expecting just what we've always gotten.
If you ask me, I'll tell you how
Faith and cynicism wrestle within us daily.
Yet we keep believing.
But would you listen?

When You Look at Me

Kate   **Imani**

When you look at me
What do you see?

                            I see my friend.

But do you see my skin?

                            I see your skin.

                            When you look at me
                            What do you see?

I see my friend.

                            But do you see my skin?

I see your skin.

Can we shed it?
Can we somehow escape?

                            I'm just trying to wear mine.
                            To be called by my name.

So how do I wear mine?
What does a friend say?

                            You ask me these questions.
                            You always love me this way.

But it's not enough.
Imani, your beauty cannot hide.

                            I'm not hiding from them, Kate.
                            It's just they keep closed their eyes.

Then we open them!
Together we make the world see.

                            It doesn't work like that.
                            Truth is whatever they believe.

No, truth is exposure,
admitting we created White and Black.
It's laying down pride and stolen dominance.
It's demanding dignity back!

(Kate)   **(Imani)**

But Kate, that's the way of your skin.
Because you wear it, you can make demands.

But it's your voice I want to raise!

I know. I've always loved you, friend, for that.

Then what? Imani?
Just tell me what to do!

Oh Kate, you're doing it.
You're loving me, and I'm loving you.

But that's not enough. *Dear God!*
Those in my skin,
they must wake up!

I didn't say that we'll be silent.
I didn't say that we'll give up.

It's just hard to see the end.

When no one will even see the start…

Who could call you
anything but friend?

Yes, in the end,
we only succeed if we change hearts.

When you look at me
What do you see?

I see my friend.

But do you see my skin?

I see your beautiful skin.

When you look at me
What do you see?

I see my friend.

But do you see my skin?

I see your beautiful skin.

Embers

Black and Blue

My Dad, My Hero (The words of **Darius's** father, a Houston police officer for over 20 years.)

Black.
Born to it
Judged for it
Draped in the excellence
As my people see it.
But History and your verdicts
Beat me for it.
Stomp on my rights
And blame me for it.
Didn't choose the skin
Just happened to be born in it.
Black like my daddy and proud of it.

Blue.
Made for it.
Judged for it.
Clouded by the prejudgment
As my community sees it,
Because of its history
And mistreatment of it.
Blamed for it.
Chose the badge
Seeking the righteousness of it.
Blue like my fellows and proud of it.

The Black and the blue of it,
Daily I balance who I am
With what I do with it.
Goodness all around me,
Both Black and blue.
Can't deny one for the other
Cause I'm true to it.
Am I too Black to be blue?
What's the truth of it?
Too blue to be Black,
What can I do with it?

How can I gauge the truth of it?
Knew there were punches thrown,
Both sides, though I never threw it.
Never saw a Black man
I wanted to die.
Two sides of the same badge
Saw the truth and the lies.
Bound by two fraternities
At odds with each other.
Black skin, blue badge each one my brother.

Divided by it.
See my opposing colors
And ask "How can you side with them?"
Blue took so many lives,
Got my Black tired of it.
Shamed by the reckless ones
On all sides of this.
Saying Black Lives Matter
Speaks to the soul of me,
But my Blue got them side-eyeing me.
Too Black to be Blue.
Too Blue to be Black.
Still got my pride in it.

When Bled

Gretchen (Gretchen's father is a retired Houston police officer.)

My daddy wore blue over White.
Your daddy wore blue over Black.
But the colors are all clashing tonight,
Staining the ground with red.

Tomorrow the smoke and the ash
Will sting a nation's sight,
Like the tear gas let loose by the blue,
We're blinded by our colors inbred.

So much said, so much burning light.
I want to feel pride for the blue,
Stand tall, next to you, against night,
But the colors lose their beauty when bled.

I Am Not This

Kate

I am White,
privileged,
American.
I am a Christian.
I am educated.
I am a southerner,
and I have eaten a lot of casseroles in my life.
But I cannot stomach this.

In the past few years,
and the last year especially,
I have tried to educate myself,
to better understand my privilege.
The more I learned,
the more gross I felt,
the more ashamed,
the more repugnant it smelled,
with deep repentance I knelt,
eager for change.

Then in an instant
the whole world *did* change.
As Covid-19 swept across every border,
both physical and racial,
across class and power structures,
it exposed our sins of ignorance and privilege.
It widened the divide between rich and poor.
Finally sweeping the doors closed
on certainty and trust.

At first,
Americans resisted the disconnection in spirit.
They found new ways to connect without forfeiting safety.
The best of humanity could be seen in snapshots,
and I dared to hope
that these were the pangs of childbirth,
and the very worst of all circumstances
might give birth to lasting change.

But it wasn't long before
the entitled beast roared
and showed his teeth.
White privilege oozed
from every mask-less face on my screen.
As the loss of comforts became too uncomfortable for the beast,
they asserted their kingly right to privilege,
or in other words—their right
to do just as they pleased.

Strangely to my ears,
I heard them call this freedom.
I puzzled at the word,
feeling the freedom to live
die a little more
with every one of their shouts.
Until I heard the cries beneath the cries,
and the lies that enable white privilege
to *deny, deny, deny.*

When comfort and ease begin to slip,
when rules and laws protect through limit,
when the right to life means less right to roam,
when the privileged tire
of their comfortable homes,
when suddenly the king
feels unfamiliarly oppressed,
be damned the limits that save the rest!

Be damned the science!
Be damned the cautions!
We are Americans, and *we* say when it's over!
We won't be told to be still!
We will keep our guns, our taxes,
and our license to kill!
But most importantly,
we'll keep our power
and assert our will.

We'll call privilege essential.
We'll call privilege freedom.
We'll claim to speak up for
the little guy,
the small business,
the essential worker.
Then we'll load our mask-less gun,
and we'll kill them all.

No, I cannot stomach this unchecked privilege.
Not even a pandemic can sway it.
Jesus hasn't yet changed it.
How could he, when we made him White?
When we used his name to protect our power?
Guess what? People were starving before Covid!
They were unemployed and needed money to feed their families.
Where was your protest then?

Now you protest freedom with tyranny.
There is nothing conservative about recklessness.
What are you conserving? And why do you call it freedom?
Freedom has never been limitless,
but it should always value
the least as much as the loudest.
Tyranny is arbitrary abuse of power.
It's the loudest overpowering the vulnerable.
It's the privilege of a few
deemed worthy of the sacrifice of many.

And we both know, you can protest like this
with your guns and your flags,
pro-law and order and the badge,
when it suits you, and all you have
Because your skin,
it isn't black.

Yes, I am White,
privileged,
American.
I am a Christian.
I am educated.
I am a southerner.
But I am not this.

Of this, I am deeply ashamed.
Something will come of this.
Something will be born from these ashes.
But first, there is so much that still must be burned.

Haikus

Aliyah

TRAUMA

Living in trauma
Wounds the soul and causes pain.
Withdraw to silence.

BECAUSE

I can't make you see,
If the price is me, my life
energy run dry.

SO NOW

Justice, I beg you,
Lend me your strong, upraised arm!
Fight for me. *For me.*

Scroll on By

Shawna

If I see you making an excuse
At the expense of a nation
And a maligned community,
Should I scroll on by?

If I see you minimizing the screams
Of my brothers
With your need to ignore,
Should I scroll on by?

Do I silently excuse myself
From a conversation
To keep the peace?
Should I scroll on by?

Does it make you uncomfortable
To see that America ain't so free
And not all are brave?
Do you scroll on by?

When you see the marching
All races and faces
Set to upend a system you hold dear,
Do you scroll on by?

When we see you soil and sully
Our revolution to preserve your
Perfect post,
Should we seek to educate you, *friend*,
Or should we scroll on by?

No Longer

Dr.

No longer polluting the air with exhaust,
we are exhausting the air with our lies.
No longer masking our pride and our hate,
we're hating masks for national pride.

No longer dying for the sake of freedom,
free men are content to let other men die.
No longer love God and love one another,
we're othering others to self-justify.

Out Out!

Gretchen, Hate, Aliyah, Nancy (June in Houston)

Gretchen

Out out!
Damn flies!
I have bleached and cleaned
And wiped all the crevices.
There is nothing dead
Or dirty,
Yet you hang out on the window
And watch me.
Why?!
Out out!

Hate

Out out!
Damn fleas!
Put your hands up high.
Keep your eyes looking down.
Protest all you want
And complain.
My knee is still on your neck.
Let 'em watch me.
Why not?!
Out out!

Aliyah

Out out!
Damn feelings!
I have cried and prayed
And marched until my feet bled.
Yet nothing has changed
Or mattered
They still see my skin as inferior
And watch me.
Why?
Out Out!

Nancy

Out out!
Damn images!
You've disturbed me today.
Made me rethink my views
Yet your presence inflames
And threatens
What I think to be true.
And you watch me.
Why now?
Out Out!

(Unfinished Art)[6]

Imani

Text Conversation:

Imani: Working on this with my chalks because I need it. It's not finished, but I love how messy making this is. The black gets everywhere.

Kate: I love this. The words, the art, the mess. And you, Imani. Beautiful.

---

[6] The exact history of the raised black fist as art and as a symbol of the Black Lives Matter movement is complicated to trace. We have sought to find the original artist to give him/her credit, but the symbol has become too ubiquitous. Instead, we offer this article as a history of the symbol and a way to understand how the symbol of the fist has risen to such familiarity and common usage. (Duffield, Charlie. "Black Lives Matter fist symbol: Meaning and history behind the Black Power raised fist salute." news.co.uk, 19 June 2020, https://www.google.com/amp/s/inews.co.uk/news/black-lives-matter-fist-symbol-meaning-black-power-history-raised-explained-432838/amp. Accessed 19 June 2020.)

Waking

Gretchen

I'm going to say the wrong things,
   and feel shame,
   and feel small;
but so be it.
I've been shamelessly big without trying
   for most all
   the days
I've had.

Unmuted

Sisters, Brothers

Using our inside voices,
Our "only Black people" voice.
Passing each other
Sharing a look.
Giving that head nod
Of acknowledgment to
All the shades of us.
That secret conversation
Saying "I see you,"
In a world where we are both
Seen and unseen,
Heard and ushered away,
Like a petulant child.
Shushed and muted
By your comments
And crumbs of acceptance.

Making you feel comfortable
Even in our discomfort,
While knowing it'll never be enough.
To be quietly bothered
And publicly muted
Kills the soul
And stirs the flames
Of discontent.
Whiplash from years of
Turning the other cheek
Simply to end up on the ground,
Sandwiched between a knee
And the street.
The screams of a community
Ignored and muted
Like background noise
On a noisy Zoom meeting.
Just an annoying bug to you
Crushed under the weight of
Endless biases
Manifesting as a self-fulfilled destiny.

A people once content
To be muted.
Pretending to be unbothered
As we sang
"We Shall Overcome"
And the "Negro National Anthem."
A people who prayed for peace
Now shout
"No Justice, No Peace!"[7]
Bothered!
Shouting!
Organizing!
Voting!
Voices raised and
Unmuted!

---

[7] The phrase, "No Justice, No Peace!" became a deafening cry in 2020, but the phrase is much older than that. Although its exact origins are not clear, it has been in use and associated with Black civil rights and specifically protests against police violence, since as early as the mid-1980's. Although this exact phrase was not used by MLK during the Civil Rights movement of the 1960's, King's words outside of a California prison on December 14, 1967, "There can be no justice without peace, and there can be no peace without justice," are often cited when the phrase is used.

Blank

Kate (Conversations with her daughter)

"Mama?"
"Yes baby."
"I want to draw with my crayons."
"What do you want to draw?"
"The world."
"The whole world?"
"The world as it should be."
"Oh, I like the sound of that."

"Baby, what do you need?"
"I have my crayons,
so just blank paper."

"Blank?"

"Yes, mama.
You know, blank paper."

"Oh baby, ...
            the paper isn't blank."

"It isn't, mama?"
"No.
The paper is white."

"But I need something blank.
Something fresh. Something clean!"
"Yes.
But that's not what you have."

"What do I have, mama?"

"You have a world that isn't blank.
A world that isn't clean.
Just like the paper.
Blank is the dream you've been taught.
But blank isn't real."

"How do I start then?
I have so much I want to draw!
But the page, it needs to be blank!
Blank needs to be real."

"You start like this.
You see the paper as it is,
and you call it by it's true name."

"And the world, mama?
What do I call the world—
a world that isn't blank?"

"You name it, too, baby.
You call it White."

Start

"How does naming it help, mama?
I don't know if I understand."

"It helps because
you cannot remake a thing,
you cannot reimagine it,
until you first know what it is.
Until you know
            —until you clearly see—
what it is that you have."

"And what I have isn't blank?"
"No, it's not."
"What I have is white?"
"Yes.
Its name is White."

"Mama?"
"Yes baby."
"Can I still do it?
If I call it by its name,
will I ever make the world…
> *different* than this?
> *better* than this?
> *beautiful like I imagined?*"

"You…
> I hope you…
> > …baby, I don't know.

…But I hope you can.
> Even more,
> > I hope that *you will*.

But the important thing
> the important thing is to START."

Darkness

Darius

Darkness is what you see
When you look at me.
It's what scares and intrigues you.
But you ignore those feelings
In the light
Because they don't fit
Who you say you are.

Darkness is what you see
When I walk into your store.
You follow me but don't
Offer assistance.
Careful to stand in lighted spaces
Believing I'm the creature of shadows,
Who you say I am.

Darkness is what you see
When I pass you on the street.
You clutch your bag tighter,
Walk faster and farther
Away from me,
Watchful, searching for the light,
Who you say you are.

Darkness is what you see
When I lie in the street.
Unbreathing, bleeding,
You offer no assistance.
Careful to claim my existence
As the criminal in need of light,
Who you think I am.

Darkness is what you see
Even when I,
Beaten, bruised, followed, and despised
Stand in the light and say
"Black Lives Matter.
My life…matters."

I am not who you say I am.
I am not who you think I am.
I cast out the
Darkness.
I am the light you see.
Not who you think I am.

I Can't Keep Quiet

Aliyah

I've been shouting and testifying
About trauma and pain.
Been swaying and rocking
To the sounds
Of "We Shall Overcome"
And "I Have a Dream."
And waving my handkerchief
As our mourning mothers
Lay across motionless
Martyred men
And women
Too loved to be forgotten,
Yet too flawed to be lifted.
Heartbroken and questioning,
"Why?"
While seeking justification and justice.
Knowing Blackness
Is the answer for one and not the other.
Seeing silence as approval,
I can't keep quiet.

Anger rolls off my skin,
Glistening in its darkness
As if to shield the grief
Of walking through a world
That sees me one way
First.
Then finds my shade of
Assimilation accepting.
At least outwardly.
Claiming me publicly,
While labeling me as a "safe one,"
A "not like the others" one.
Until I speak up and speak out about the duplicity
I see as I walk in Blackness.
I tire of keeping quiet and calm,
Concerned that I'll be labeled an "angry one."
Knowing Blackness
Is now the reason I shout.
No more silence for approval.
I can't keep quiet.

Fall to Pieces

Imani

> "When things were going great
> I crowed, 'I've got it made.
> I'm God's favorite.
> He made me King of the mountain.'
> Then you looked the other way
> and I fell to pieces."
> (*MSG* Ps. 30.6-7)[8]

A few days ago, I read Psalm 30, and it came alive to me. When I read verses 6 and 7, I could see it. A mountain, strong and tall, high above everything and everyone else. But this mountain, which prided itself on rightness and light, found itself in darkness. God had turned his face away from the mountain because in its power it had forgotten justice. The mountain, separated from God, finally began to crumble and repent.

I sat in that shadow a while. Contemplating the weight of it. The fear, the sorrow. The uncertainty and longing for hope.

---

[8] Peterson, Eugene H. *The Message*. Colorado Springs, CO: NavPress, 2002. Print.

Whirling Dance

Imani

Then I read verses 11-12, and again, I could see it. The wild lament of the oppressed, the broken, the exhausted in the valley, raising our voices to God and being heard. Being seen. Being bathed in beautiful light as our lament was turned into whirling dance. As our tear-stained stories and strivings were adorned with wildflowers, and our cries became a song that shook the crumbling mountain to its knees.

In those verses I was also surprised by a staggering HOPE. Because from the rubble, the mountain also cried a wild lament. And God turns wild lament into whirling dance! And I could see it. The mountain AND the valley moving, singing, and beautiful. I haven't been able to get these images out of my mind.

"You did it: You changed wild lament
into whirling dance;
you ripped off my black mourning band
and decked me with wildflowers.
I'm about to burst with song;
I can't keep quiet about you.
God, My God,
I can't thank you enough."
(*MSG* Ps. 30.11-12)[9]

---

[9] Peterson, Eugene H. *The Message*. Colorado Springs, CO: NavPress, 2002. Print.

No One Said It Would Be Easy

Kate

To live like Jesus is hard.
It doesn't happen where they told me it would.
It doesn't happen beneath a pristine steeple.
It doesn't happen in matching T-shirts.

To love like Jesus is hard.
Hate now walks around in the daylight.
Shamelessly declaring its prior claim to Christ.
Painting my brown Savior American, rich, and so pale.

To see like Jesus is hard.
The loudest voices insist the world is Black, White, and colorblind, all at once.
And a powerful evil bullies us backwards,
openly striving to make America's past wrongs right again.

To heal like Jesus is hard.
So many live with open bleeding wounds they deny exist.
Rot and decay fester there and the stench accosts the marginalized.
Yet who can heal disease, renamed and reinvigorated as patriotism and national
    pride?

To die like Jesus is hardest.
To lay myself down outside of my comfortable living room,
in places where I am other and exposed,
to be hated as He was hated by my own, such as this—it's hard.

But silence is just another nail,
another nail in the very hands of the Jesus
who I must follow,
even in this death.

Cowards Behind Keyboards

Aliyah

You picked a good one
For you.
An article, quote, or meme
That fit just right,
For you.
One that had very little merit,
No facts
Yet served the purpose to distract,
For you.
Shifted from the symptoms and illness
To the destruction. It worked
For you.
Cowardly conversations
Without revelations,
Amongst those who think
Like you
Serve to hide the growth
Of your alliances
And biases
Until the cancer spreads,
Through you.

I Always Know I'm Black

Shawna

You don't see skin color.
That's some shit you say.
Unrealistic at best.
A lie at worst.
It's the collateral you offer
As the security for your privilege,
So, you can ignore
That part of me that makes you uncomfortable in your comfort.
You think it makes you "woke."
Though you're slumbering on how that statement makes you blind
To the inequality and inequities
My color affords me
In our shared spaces
And those places I don't quite fit.

The "they" and "them" and even the "those people" don't slip
From your lips as often.
Consciousness contrived,
You've reserved those titles for
"Them" who march,
"Those" who live on your street,
But aren't invited to the party.
And "those people" who play their music too loud
And often want to stand out in the crowd.
You know "they" vote Democrat
Since "they" want a hand out
Because "they" are lazy.
What about when "they" use the race card
To shut down the conversation?
I don't want to fit into those places.

I always know I'm Black.
It greets me in the mirror
And gives life to the vibrant color of my hair and clothing.
It colors my outlook on all things
Yet is not an excuse to escape anything.
It's the fire under my feet
And the feeling in my gut as I hold my breath praying that

The "they" you speak of aren't Black.
It's pride and pursuit of excellence,
While being weighed down with the responsibility of an entire community.
"Work 100 times harder to get half the rewards" reminder passed from generation
to the next.
Resolved to excel because I represent so many.
It's who I am.
I fit into that place
—Black.

Black Lives Matter

Imani[10]

Text Conversation:

Imani: Finished.

If only I could draw on hearts.

Kate: Yes. If only…

---

[10] *See* footnote 6.

Oxygen to a
Flame

Juneteenth

Darius (June 19, 2020)

Yes, I celebrate July 4th.
Proud American citizen, for what it's worth.
Never a day have forsaken red, white, and blue,
I've even popped firecrackers and barbecued.
Partied with friends and family and enjoyed the day off.
Even recall patriotic lessons from school
About what America's freedom cost.
I've celebrated the country with pride on many occasions.
I'll never deny, America is a great nation.
But as important as the 4th is to this country,
Shackles, whips, and chains bought my entry.

"My country 'tis of thee"[11]
Sweet land of slavery…
July 4th pales in comparison to thee,
The day that means the world to me,
The 19th of June—
Juneteenth.

I celebrate Jubilee Day.
June 19th 1865… Emancipation Day!
The day southern enslaved men, women, and children
Were told of their freedom.
Though Lincoln's proclamation gave way to a day to remember,
1862, the 22nd of September,
Only those slaves in Northern states received it's due.
The 13th Amendment, abolishing slavery took some time to go through.
Those confederate states still had their way.
Slavery was theirs until Freedom Day.
Freedom ain't free and freed men weren't free.
They weren't yet granted equality and equity
or even the right to just be.

---

[11] Smith, Samuel Francis. "America (My Country 'Tis of Thee)." 1832.

"My country 'tis of thee"
Sweet land of slavery…
July 4th pales in comparison to thee,
The day that means the world to me,
The 19th of June—
Juneteenth.

We Will Keep

Hate (June 20, 2020, Trump Rally, Tulsa, Oklahoma)

Slow down the testing!
With force, take the streets!
Our confederate monuments,
with pride, we will keep!
We'll ridicule with gusto,
let hate light the match.
Then burn all your strivings,
'til your dreams, too, are black.

Gray

Nancy

It's all black and white—
and the edges too close.
One drop of the one,
and the other's undone.
For clear lines there's no hope.

November is coming.
The virus is still here.
Race is still rioting.
Over masks we're still fighting.
Why is nothing now clear?

It was easy before—
my vote cast for me.
For the unborn child's rights,
the choice black and white,
now there's men who can't breathe.

How did we get to this place?
Where my vote can't be godly?
If I care about the economy,
I don't care about their poverty.
When did my choice become so costly?

I admit, I miss the clarity—
a divided world of black and white.
Where I didn't know division scarred;
I could be proud of who we are;
I'd never lived this gray of night.

Blacks Like You

Belinda

George Floyd is not a hero to me, nor
Is he a martyr for me to march for.
He was accused of committing a crime.
He was simply out of line.
He should've put his hands behind his back.
Civilized people who did no wrong
Don't act like that.
Black people have it so much better than we've ever had it.
I don't subscribe to the concept that we are oppressed.
We are being sold lies, nothing less.
It's the media and their twisted view.
They do a disservice to White people and Black people, too.

I've read all the books by Blacks
Who say we are not oppressed, that we are far from that.
I support their view and no others.
I do not see all Blacks as sisters and brothers.
Many Black people cater to the view of reparations.
While they should be thinking about their salvation.
They should be happy to be here in the land of the free and the brave.
They have got to stop thinking like the runaway slave.
Black people are the only people who want justice for criminals up to no good.
When they should be trying to educate themselves, not burn their neighborhoods.
You would have to search far and look wide
To find a Jew, or White, or even a Latino who'll fight on the criminal's side.
But Blacks will fight and march for the least of us, it's true.
So, I must distance myself from Blacks like you.

Can't Even Have a Drink

J.R. (June 25, 2020)[12]

Can't even have a drink.
Widow who owns Jack's now
Won't open her doors.
Expects customer loyalty I'm sure.
She's bought into all the fear.
Where's her faith in the good Lord?
You can't eat in a mask,
She can't pay bills without cash,
Will she starve for their war?

Because we all need a drink
And a good meal with friends.
This virus ain't gonna wipe us out,
Most of the looting is over now,
We can't stop our lives for this!
City's listenin' to that county judge.
Liberal liar talks too damn much,
For caution she'd make us poor.

Shit, I just need a drink.
My bar to be open again,
My boy, Darius, pouring my whiskey
—Smart kid making tips off the tipsy—
News up and the world looking normal,
Exhale all the fear liberals sell me.
No more marching, no masks,
No more bitchin', just my glass,
Me at Jack's, and this nightmare no more.

---

[12] Despite the ability for Texas restaurants to reopen at 25% and then 50%, and then on June 12, 2020, at 75%, Jack's is a small restaurant with limited seating already, so Shawna has waited, pivoting to take-out instead. On June 25, 2020, Governor Abbot of Texas pushed his Reopen Texas Plan, despite strong resistance from Harris County Judge, Lina Hidalgo. Then one day later, June 26th, Abbot had to reverse course, once again closing bars and dropping restaurants back to 50% as Covid-19 cases in Texas began to dramatically rise.

We Are

Darius (June 28, 2020)[13]

Shawna is opening the patio bar.
I understand. Rent is due.
The quickest payday requires booze.
Lord knows I need the money to pay for school,
So this is where we are,

But I've marched so far.
Don't know if this time I can serve those fools.
Hollerin' for me to turn up Fox News,
With all their bullshit, I think I'm through.
They don't see my scars.

Don't know who we are.
They'll never know who we are.

---

[13] Governor Abbot issued a special waiver for Texas bars to sell premixed drinks to-go. Shawna makes the decision to open the patio bar for to-go orders from both the bar and the restaurant. The outdoor patio will also offer a small amount of socially distanced outdoor seating.

Heavy

Shawna

Today, I'm feeling heavy.
Heavy with hurt,
Heavy with anger,
Heavy with disappointment.
Too heavy to smile at customers
And fill glasses,
And feign interest in their orders.
The tears too heavy to reside inside,
Force themselves down my face.
Heavy on my chin,
Heavy in my heart.
But I mask my face,
Force a smile,
Fill the glasses,
And hide the heavy.

Masked Heroes Fight Villains

Aliyah (As a Saharan dust storm descends on Houston. Aliyah writes frustrated Haikus.)[14]

Covid-19 you
are a bitch, such a bitch. Wait!
Let me get my mask.

                    Racism on my
                    screen. March! We ain't your bitch. No!
                    Let me get my mask.

          Saharan dust you
          are a bitch, such a bitch. Wait!
          Let me get my mask.

                    White supremacists
                    sittin' high. Hold up, bitches,
                    I'll tear off your masks.

---

[14] Aliyah woke up to an epic Saharan dust storm descending on Houston and irritating her lungs when she was already struggling to catch her breath.

I Can't

Kate

Bite me!
2020,
Trump cronies,
this feeling lonely.
Suck it!
Covid uptick,
racist bigots,
Fox News phonies.
Fuck you!
Saharan dust plume,
loss of safe schools
and ceremonies.
I can't.
Within this wasteland,
breathe this damn sand,
or hopeless owns me.

Night Air

Nancy (July 2, 2020, Statewide face-covering requirement issued.)[15]

How different the night air is,
breathing air through this mask.
Just last week, I never wore one.
Now it's required, and I want to ask:
What was the fight for?
Why did you tell us to guard our freedom?
What were we freed from,
If now you tell me that I need them?
If this was the place we were headed,
why didn't we start here way back then?
How many dead people now would be breathing,
if we had been breathing night air like this,
All along?
       ...and what else have we gotten wrong?

---

[15] Governor Abbot of Texas, after prohibiting counties from enforcing mask orders, finally establishes a statewide face-covering requirement.

On Broadway

Dr. (July 3, 2020, *Hamilton* is released on Disney+ for the July 4th weekend.)

Daydreams. Nightmares.
Our settings have shifted,
the casting reduced,
the plots redirected.
Now days marked by stillness
and nights ruled by fear,
should reawaken some longings,
should compel hearts to hear.
But pandemic reworking,
rewriting, recasting,
has left too many actors
time for restless broadcasting.
Opinions Trump facts,
valued higher than thinking.
With intellect dying,
we're reduced to poor tweeting.
But I'm willing to fully
fund Hamilton's Broadway.
Don masks and our dignity,
take the iron rod away.
Recast the Chief
of a sinking production.
With a few heaps of humility,
reverse our dysfunction.
For I am a patron
of our theatre and art,
but this ruckus on stage,
it is breaking my heart.

Born to Lead

J.R.'s oldest son, Ty

J.R.'s oldest son

I keep climbing,
but the ladder is changing.
I keep tryin',
but this sidelining's enraging.
This ain't the way I was raised,
ain't made to play this new game.
Born to lead in this land
outsiders are claiming.

Fourth of July
is my favorite holiday.
red, blue, and the White
is my right, under God I pray.
In the land of the free,
we make our way.
Born to lead in this land
they don't want to keep the same.

My father's a patriot,
hardworking, honest man.
But now the immigrant
wants to take it from his hand.
He longs for the way it used to be.
I long for any way that remains for me.
Born to lead in this land
where men have forgotten how we stay free.

Ty

Disillusioned,
by birthrights and exclusion.
You are right,
because the right, to be right
is your foregone conclusion.
Forget giftings that are natural.
My God-given intelligence just baffles.
My only right is to be wrong,
until my exceptionalism's gone,
an inconvenient intrusion.

True equality,
parsed out, leads to your despondency.
If equal means that I can be best,
it also means you could be less,
and that disrupts your hierarchy.
But it's not my weakness you despise.
Instead, my brilliance can't meet your eyes.
If I dare step out of my caste,
you make damn sure I am the last.
Ever preserving *your* American democracy.

July 4th

Ty (Watching the Trump campaign's July 4th event at Mount Rushmore, South Dakota, from his T.V. in Houston.)

I see your fireworks displaying your dominance,
Like cannons erupting in powerful obstinance
To celebrate a holiday of your independence.
White men as the backdrop, I see your indifference.
Still you feign honor on stolen land.
On sacred Black Hills carved White you stand.
Saluting a flag and a day for White men,
For who else had rights and freedoms back then?
Yet who am I, to point out that slaves
Who fought in your war, woke up still in chains?
July 4th was to them, no more than reminder
That Jefferson's "all" remained a divider.
For slaves were not men, to your forefathers.
Sure, Lincoln was different, but Johnson resolved it.
It's two-thousand and twenty, yet I am still here,
Watching mighty displays, instilling new fears.
For that's your campaign, "Make America HATE again,"
Mask-less oppressors, *Lord!* You better not win.

Cover Me

Aliyah

According to tradition
Those colors stand for more than sedition.
The symbol of a nation
Unified in its intention
To represent democracy.
Does it cover me?

White stripes for the purity and innocence
Of people wanting equal representation.
Yet they practiced trafficking of an entire population
Of people who received no equality,
And were pure and innocent in their desire to be free.
Do those stripes cover me?

Red stripes for the hardiness and valor
Granted them freedom and autonomy.
Yet shackles and segregated laws
Became the greatest flaws
Of the great experiment I see.
Do those stripes cover me?

Blue signifies vigilance, perseverance, and justice.
We, Americans, are quick to take a stand
To support people of other lands.
Warring for justice and civil rights
Yet on our shores we have oversight.
Does the canton cover me?

Black, they say, conjures darkness, evil, and threatens a few.
But its richness and sophistication, I wish they knew.
All the colors need its presence for depth and variation.
It's intricately woven into the fabric of this nation,
Even if the flag shows no representation.
And it covers me.

Flag

Gretchen, J.R., Aliyah, Nancy

Gretchen

They burned the flag today.
The flames climbed so high,
licking arms of light
across the sky,
and I held my breath
with unblinking eyes.
I beheld the death
of my simplistic life.

J.R.

They burned the flag today.
The flame hot, like my rage
for their disrespect,
for young, foolish games
others fought to protect.
But they think they're brave,
to live out a freedom their flames forget.

Aliyah

They burned the flag today.
I never imagined
I'd be there to witness,
To raise my arms high,
Screaming, "See me! LISTEN!"
With a heart broken, soul lost,
Declaring my country unforgiven.
Struggling to believe this America
can ever be rewritten.

Nancy

They burned the flag today.
Flames high on every screen.
My phone declaring with every ring,
all the usual suspects swearing, and baiting me,
but I, for one, could not unsee
a girl, I knew, there in the streets.
Tearstained and lost, arms raised up high,
did we make her cry? Did we cause her grief?

Because Aliyah burned the flag today!
Our symbol of American freedom.
Calling that America a lie.
Calling for America to be remade.
From Blue flame.
Red heat.
White Ash.
Reborn.

Scream

Aliyah

I'm shaking.
They burned a flag today.
Though I didn't light the match,
I was there.
I screamed from somewhere deep in my belly
And lodged in my being.
It was a release I didn't know I needed.
I'm heartbroken, still.
Conflicted and guilty
About what I feel for this country
And how they treat me, and
People who look like me.
They see me, but I also see myself.

There was no victory today.
That scream that came out of nowhere,
Those arms held high
Now fill me with shame.
For what I've seen.
What I've done and
What I feel—conflicted
I'm lost, still.
This anger is inside me.
Though I love my country,
I'm struggling to believe
In those colors
Those stripes
That flag.
I'm crying, still.
The disappointment in myself,
In that flag
In this movement
In that match
In my country,
Revealed in that scream.
They see me, and I also see myself.

The Fall of Capitalism

J.R.

Deception is slow,
meticulous work.
It takes patience discreet,
to change a nation's heartbeat.
You choose your moment; you choose your words.
Ahh…
You see their poets, they are skilled.
With a knife they write change.
They will take what is true,
they will sacrifice you,
until exceptionalism is slain.
Yes…
By raising black lives,
they will lower common man.
With their Marxist ideals,
equalizing appeals,
they'll take all from your hand.
Now…
I agree, God loves the meek,
but the meek, they are not.
Over George Floyd they rejoiced,
made a calculated choice,
to loot America for all we've got.

Please, Consider, on the Topics of...

Will

Privilege

Privilege is a four-letter word,
when aimed at your village
nothing's gained, nothing's heard.
"Blessed" is much more popular—
captioning our mantels, our tables, our coffers.
But might we consider the inverse of that thought?
Is to be Black, to be scorned by our God?
I do not believe he abhors his creation.
Maybe privileged is, in fact, our true station.

BLM

#blacklivesmatter I hear you call Marxist,
fearing White lives be eclipsed by their darkness.
But we worship a God, who himself is pure light:
Spotlighting their march and hearing their plight.
Where is this darkness you see rolling in?
I see only light piercing darkness, exposing sin.
For the poor for the sick, Jesus came.
Because their lives matter, he chose to be slain.
Will you let go these convenient excuses?
Will you recognize more than yesterday's nooses?
Because real oppression is not easily slain,
Not when systems assure it, and we refuse to bear blame.
Oppression masquerades, as a son of light.
Painting its darkness a bright shiny White.
            ...and you might excommunicate me for speaking this truth,
            even though you taught me that this is what I should do...

Brave Free

Imani

~~Land of the free~~
       ~~free to speak anything;~~
       ~~free to believe anything;~~
       ~~free to achieve anything;~~
       ~~free to dream anything.~~

Land of the free—
       free to speak like you;
       free to believe like you;
       free to achieve *if* you;
       free to dream *if* you.

~~Home of the brave~~
       ~~brave to expose the hatred;~~
       ~~brave to name the hatred;~~
       ~~brave to repent of the hatred;~~
       ~~brave to change the hatred.~~

Home of the brave—
       brave to display your rightness;
       brave to name it righteousness;
       brave to repent all weakness;
       brave to change Lord Jesus.

Powerless

J.R., Darius, Gretchen

J.R.

Powerless.
They say "No justice. No Peace."
Yet every right that's been given to me,
they have it too, yet they say they're not free?
And still they want more?
They are tearing down our history.
Chant by chant, monuments crumble.
Yet they say *I'm* the one who stumbles!
Because I've built wealth, now I cannot be humble?
They'd make America a welfare state,
but what about *my* children's welfare?
They'll have so much in taxes to repay,
that all I've built will be taken away.

> *Like my thoughts,*
> *like my words,*
> *snatched away,*
> *and dismissed—*

as old fashioned and cruel,
the xenophobia of a fool.
They say I'm exclusive, misogynistic,
that I'm a privileged, male supremacist,
I must be brainwashed and unintelligent.
Unchristian racist, now that's my favorite.

But none of it's true!
That's not who I am.
Yet all that they do,
their platform, their plan,
it edges me out,
the very sound of my voice.
It erases my dreams, my hopes, and my choice!
Does what I value
have no value? To anyone
in all this noise?

There is no middle ground,
no compromise.
We must win in November,
or they'll silence our cries,
      and leave us
            Powerless.

Darius

Powerless.
They take our protest and call it riot.
Arrest another "Black man,"
keep him nameless, to hide it.
Carry guns on capital steps,
because they ain't free? Hell no, with their shit!
From safety and health, they want emancipation?
Well I'm coming at them with a proclamation:
You're so free, you don't know what free is!
So supreme, can't say I should live!
If you fear masks will rob you of freedom,
if your own scientists, you don't believe 'em,
how fast will you shut me down? How fast will I hit the ground?

> *Like my thoughts,*
> *like my words,*
> *snatched away,*
> *and dismissed—*

as angry bullshit, armed and dangerous,
of a thieving bastard, immoral, not like us.
Oh, am I whining, exaggerating?
A liberal mouthpiece, elaborating?
Am I just brainwashed and uninformed?
A fatherless criminal who needs the Lord?

But none of it's true!
That's not who I am.
Yet all that you do,
your platform, your plan,
it edges me out,
the very sound of my voice.
It erases my dreams, my hopes, and my choice!
Does what I value
have no value? To anyone
in all this noise?

There is no middle ground,
no compromise.
We must win in November,
or they'll silence our cries,
and leave us
Powerless.

Gretchen

Powerless.
Take my Jesus and call him a Republican.
Take systematic racism
and call it blessing from above.
See I'm pro-life for the unborn _and_ the Black man.
I have no home for my heart in this vacuum
of raging politics and derisive schism.
God of heaven, call us to repentance!
I will no longer be told what to think.
Church, you got him wrong, my Jesus, my King!
He's more than just telling me I am forgiven.
He's about justice and bringing his kingdom from heaven!
Yet you'll disregard me as false religion.

Like my thoughts,
like my words,
snatched away,
and dismissed—

as liberal lies, tainted unholy,
as the fallen away, who let the culture mold me.
If I am vocal, I'm virtue casting.
If I'm inclusive, heaven won't have me.
If I vote Democrat, I'm no longer Christian.
If I vote my conscience, to my naivety I've given in.
But none of it's true!
That's not who I am.
Yet all that you do,
your platforms, your plans,
They all edge me out,
the very sound of my voice.
They erase my dreams, my hopes, and my choice!
Does what I value
have no value? To anyone
in all this noise?

>There is no middle ground,
>no compromise.
>Whoever wins in November,
>will they silence my cries,
>and leave me
>Powerless?

Cost of Character

Kate

This November, could we set parties aside?
Forsake policy for national pride?
The cost is character, if we should fail.
Are there any of us, who want to look down that trail?
Haven't we forsaken too much character already?
Can we be done with the shouting and being petty?
I want my children to know what "Presidential" means.
It sure isn't there in this bully's tweets.

Our Women

Ty (August 11, 2020, Kamala Harris is named Biden's Vice-Presidential pick.)

So, a White man has declared
A woman of color to be fit,
As his second in command,
His diversity and shit.
And I want to raise my fist
In solidarity and triumph,
But it's hard to believe that this
Will mean a fuck to their defiance.
They'll call her angry 'cause she's Black,
Call her a man when she wears pants.
They'll only see what she might lack,
Her accomplishments be damned.
Do they know that it's our women
Who have shouldered our every man,
Every child, and every burden,
Every death by pale White hands?
Our women are fierce, and they are bold!
If they are angry, they have every right.
They are resilient, they are powerful,
and I have been blessed to know their might.

Semantic Satiation

Dr.

Sometimes words lose their meaning,
from repetition or senseless tweeting.
Is your semantic satiation fleeting?
Because mine won't go away.

"Conservative" is what they say,
yet conservation ain't their jam,
unless it's conserving freedom to not give a damn.
So wait, what *does* Conservative mean?

And I thought "Liberal" could *not* conserve,
yet they consistently follow the experts' word,
conserving people, populations, and earth.
So wait, what *does* Liberal mean?

Maybe it all makes sense to you.
Maybe you can love Jesus and live selfish, too.
Ignoring the marginalized and truth,
would conserve your energy and power, too.

You'd end your semantic satiation,
redefining Conservative with your justifications.
I guess it really is great to be you:
Reality doesn't have to affect what you do!

Lightning

Aliyah

It's
thundering
Outside.
Inside.
Everywhere.

And the lightning is close
With blinding,
Destructive
Despair.

But what will it strike?
Out there?
In here?
In me?

Is this really our only light?
In storm.
In darkness.

Unfree.

People Like You

J.R.   **Ty**

People like you
always making excuses.
Can't pull up your bootstraps and make a life.
Instead you'd rather
thieve, loot, shoot, and fight.
Who else reacts like this, blowin' fuses?

People like you
revel in our violence.
Smug ass sits back and turns up your T.V.
You exclaim,
"Look at them, and you will see!"
You never take a beat for silence.

People like you
have every opportunity,
but Democrats shackled you with welfare.
Your men in the pen,
or gone off elsewhere.
No wonder you're impoverished in perpetuity!

People like you
don't listen with ears to hear.
You only listen for confirmation,
that people like me
make our own damnation.
Won't validate a <u>single</u> tear.

(J.R.)   **(Ty)**

People like you
ain't ever gonna change.
Too hooked on your drugs, your gangs, and lazy.
Yet I ain't "PC"
and Conservative is crazy??
When did law and values become estranged?

People like you
play up fragile innocence.
Act like your knee ain't on my neck!
Absolved by promises
writ like bad checks.
'Cept of *your* America I still ain't a citizen.

People like you
won't be satisfied,
until you destroy the America I love.
Patriotism and exceptionalism will die,
still it will never be enough.
Until our greatness is squandered, over a past decried.

People like you
won't be satisfied,
unless your supremacy remains intact.
Unless you hoard wealth
built upon our backs.
Be damned the truth, long-as you keep your pride.

I *despise* people like you.

I *despise* people like you.

Wildfires

Dr. (Late August, September)[16]

California is burning.
Hot
licking flames.
This hell keeps on turning.
Hot
degrading hate.
The virus is raging.
Wild
unrestrained.
Hope? It's all fading.
Wildfires
and plague.

---

[16] Wildfires were raging across California, endangering people and homes.

I Dissent

Aliyah (September 18, 2020, Supreme Court Justice Ruth Bader Ginsburg died and a nation mourned. RIP RBG.)

Guilty
until proven innocent.
I dissent.
Lazy
and discontent.
I dissent.
Welfare
handouts misspent.
I dissent.
Fatherless bastards
we could prevent.
I dissent.
To all authority
malcontent.
I dissent.
Unremarkable
by own consent.
I dissent.
Exaggerate
grievances invent.
I dissent.
Sit back while you breathe
without repent.
I dissent.

Jack's

Shawna (September 21, 2020, Governor Abbot of Texas allows restaurants to open to 75% capacity once more.)

I had to reopen.
At first just the patio bar.
I feel sick and irresponsible,
what if my people come to harm?
But my people are being plundered,
whether I open my doors or not.
The world has not been kind.
We are worn and we are scarred.

Why

Darius (September 22, 2020, Covid death toll in the U.S. passes 200,000; September 23, 2020, Grand jury fails to indict three Louisville Metro Police Department Officers for killing Breonna Taylor.)

Why did I think you'd care if I died?
200,000 lost and you haven't cried.
More fall every day on every side.
Why did I think you'd care if I died?

Wait for It

Sisters (September 23, 2020)

Wait for it.
That's what we did.
Waited for the indictment
That did nothing but punctuate
The worth they assigned her life.

Wait for it.
That's what we did.
Clairvoyant, we knew before the words
Were stoically uttered.
'Cause ain't nothing new to our strife.

Wait for it.
That's what we did.
A mockery; the justice the walls received
But our sister's life
Was a casualty of chance.

Wait for it.
That's what we did.
Hoping, but filled with the cynicism
Of the justice, unbalanced
And slanted against Black lives.

Wait for it.
That's what we did.
The salty tears of "not again" cascade down
Mixed with the hot anger of knowing
A hashtag will accentuate another Black name.

Wait for it.

Breonna Taylor

Gretchen (September 23, 2020)

Breonna Taylor.
Her name is welling in my heart.
Breonna Taylor.
Shot and grieved, lives torn apart.
Breonna Taylor.
When there's no justice, there is no peace.
Breonna Taylor.
Her flame extinguished has lit in me
Breonna Taylor.
a light that burns now in my soul.
Breonna Taylor.
I'll speak your name; the world will know.
Breonna Taylor.
No indictments? I have conviction.
Breonna Taylor.
Lord! Won't be another forgotten victim.

Come March With Me

Aliyah

You saw the video.
This one touched your soul.
Which tapped into the mother in you,
The humanity in you,
The Christian in you.
Before that moan echoed,
Your privilege insulated you
From Powerlessness,
Helplessness,
Blackness.
Come march with me.

You've listened to us speak.
Heard of countless injustices
Which touched your Americanness,
The righteous in you,
The patriot in you.
You've heard the battle cry
Of a community you now
Have empathy for,
Want justice for,
Feel the fire burning for.
Come march with me.

You've seen us weep
And could no longer look away.
Which stirred the emotions in you,
The fearlessness in you,
The power in you.
You've read books
To learn and understand
The pain, fear, anger, and
Distrust.
You embrace my humanity.
Come march with me.

We've Come a Long Way

Aliyah's Mama, Aliyah (A conversation between Aliyah and her mother one day after the Breonna Taylor decision. Aliyah is joining protesters in the streets.)

Aliyah's Mama   **Aliyah**

We've come a long way,
No longer enslaved.
No shackles, no chains.
No 'Massa' calling our name.
Don't work in the fields
From dawn 'til dusk.
Don't have to hide our intelligence
'Cause 'Massa' won't trust.
Don't have to follow the drinking gourd
Or cry out to the Lord,
Singing "Swing Low Sweet Chariot."
Freedom is what we got.

> Yet, Mamas still cry.
> Sons taken away
> And didn't say goodbye.
> Still ain't free.

We've come a long way,
No more following the North Star.
No more disguising who we are.
Since the great
Emancipation Proclamation
That some say divided a nation.
13th, 14th, 15th Amendments.
None really ended it,
Not the separateness
Of the races,
But freedom is what we got.

> Yes, but we are still killed in the streets.
> A Black man, and justice, seldom meet.
> Courts and cops don't see
> White and Black the same.
> Born and die with a hashtag
> by our name.
> Still ain't free.

(Aliyah's Mama)   **(Aliyah)**

Still, we've come a long way.
Jim Crow don't follow wherever we go.
Crosses don't burn in our yards no more.
We got the right to vote across the nation,
And ain't no legalized segregation.
Dr. King, boycotts, Rosa Parks,
Marches, and Supreme Court decisions
Were a spark.
To ignite equality
In this country.
Freedom is what we got.

> Crosses don't burn, but our anger boils over,
> About the death of yet another brother.
> Tired of recovering from heartbreak.
> It's our humanity and equity at stake.
> Tired of all the systemic excuses
> And all the abuses.
> Still ain't free.

We've come a long way.
Through so much, we've come so far.
So many firsts distinguish who we are.
Historically Black colleges and universities,
Lawyers, astronauts, doctors,
And the first
Black Supreme Court Justice—

> Yet, STILL NO JUSTICE!

> I know we've come a long way, Mama.
> None of that erases the hate and the drama.
> Our people have endured and excelled
> in spite of injustice, Mama.
> Hell, I cried and praised with you
> at the election of President Obama.
> But I can't overlook
> that my brothers and sisters still die today.
> They still die, Mama, and justice looks away.

(Aliyah's Mama)   **(Aliyah)**

Whether it's party lines, race divides, denying
Black Lives Matter
While shouting support for blue lives.
Pointing fingers at Black victims,
both men and women.
That's why I march, Mama.
That's why I can't give in.
That's why the tears roll down my face.
Mama, I know we've come a long way.
But for Breonna, for them, for Son, for us,
there is no justice today!
Can't you see?
We've come a long way, but
Still ain't free.

I see what you see
and mourn every day.
For her, for them, for Son,
for us, I pray.
Aliyah, God hasn't forgotten us.
My faith still leads the way.
I know we still ain't free,
but Aliyah,
We've come a *mighty* long way.

Mighty indeed.
400 years of days and marching feet
And yet—
We still ain't free.
Mama, we still ain't free.

If God Was a Woman

Shawna (Shawna in her restaurant after the Breonna Taylor decision. She is deeply upset by the verdict and is considering joining protesters in the streets.)

If God was a woman
Would Her wails
Wake the wounded from Her womb?
Would She whisper
"Wake my son"?
Would She block bullets
Blindly bolting through bellies?

If God was a woman
Would She condemn the culprits?
Would She demand dignity denied?
Would She crawl to cover the
Bloody bodies sprawled in the
Street, shielding them from
Shots silencing shouts?

If God was a woman
Would the walls wonder why
They received justice when
Her daughter was denied?
Would the jury justify the deficiency of jurisprudence?
Or purposefully ponder the
Pandering of the police or the people?

If God was a woman
Would She drape the damaged
Over Her bare breast?
Or would She chastise Her children?
Would Her cries cover a collapsed corpse?
Or would She march mightily with
Posters protesting police profiling?

Echoes in the Night

Gretchen

We know your name.
We remember.
We grieve.
We demand justice
for your life.

Aliyah

You are beloved,
missed,
unforgotten.
A battle cry,
and a spark,
for a movement
overdue.

Dr.

Different sides
of the same flag,
still stare in awe
at the shadow it casts.

Ty
Show me
a person
fighting for justice
for all,
and I'll show you
a patriot.

Shawna

Vocally outraged
by protestors.
But suspiciously silent
about the death
of a man.
Be careful to be
on the right side of justice.

Imani

I long for an America
as promised.
Land of the free.
Home of the brave.

Will

America is her best,
when her promises
are kept.

Darius

I'm tired
of demanding
justice.
When justice
should light the way.

Kate

As we wage
this uncivil
war,
we must be careful
to remake,
America's
broken parts.

Mama

He **wouldn't want**
to be **remembered**
this way.

Debatable

Kate (September 29, 2020, First Presidential Debate)

Tuesday night
There were words.
>There was little,
>And a lot,
>That was heard.

"Stand back.
Stand by."[17]
>Hate and fear
>Will do their job
>And divide.

Made up minds,
At the start,
>Came to watch
>A dream
>Be torn apart.

America—
Reduced to acronym:
>**U**-nwavering
>**S**-elf important
>**A**-rrogance.

No level of acumen
Left in the ring.
>Is this us?
>Two old White dudes
>Fighting?

Are we more?
Or are we them?
>Interrupting.
>No one listening.
>No one wins.

I'm backing Biden.
He has my sympathy.
>Trump has less integrity
>Than any President
>In history.

---

[17] Trump, Donald. "Presidential Debate." *Election 2020*. Moderated by Chris Wallace, Sheila and Eric Samson Pavilion, Cleveland, Ohio: NBC News, 29 Sept. 2020. Television.

But I wanted more.
I wanted it all.
    I wanted unity.
    I wanted purple,
    The old guard to fall.
The Statue of Liberty,
She isn't green.
    She is brown.
    She is female.
    She is clean.
Last night was filth.
Blood on our hands.
    Trump is our fault.
    He is our voice.
    He is this land.
But I refuse,
To let that stick.
    I refuse
    To let my children
    Remember this.
Maybe 2020
Can't be redeemed,
    But for their futures,
    I will hold on
    To better dreams.

The Fall

Dr.

Is this America or Rome?
Is Odoacer at the helm?
Did I miss the overthrow?
'Cause it's barbarian as hell.

Is this America or Greece?
No Alexanders to unite.
Once known for grand democracy,
we conquer nothing, just divide.

Is this America or Egypt?
Our New Kingdom's no longer new.
Instead of building we're declining.
Maybe this experiment is through.

Scorched

2020 Vision

Will

This sunrise is magnificent.
Surreal.
Breathtaking.
And I need to be captivated.
Astounded.
I need something to look toward.
To look up.
Something to see.

My eyes are tired.
My vision strained.
Too much ache, anger,
too much pain.
How is 2020 the world
in which we wake?
It's hard to hope,
in the newness
of each day.

Let this light correct
in me what's blurred.
Bring into focus
steps to take,
what to unlearn.
Fill my mouth, my heart,
my soul!
With truth and courage
to see your light
in this unknown.

Cascading Light

Imani (Ps. 36.9)[18]

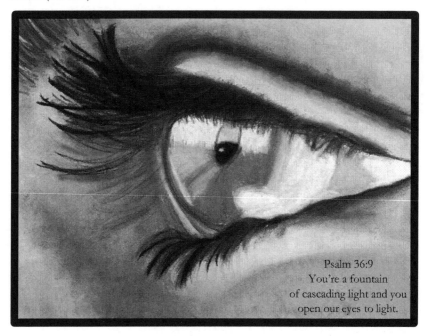

Psalm 36:9
You're a fountain
of cascading light and you
open our eyes to light.

Kate

I'm exhausted from darkness. I need light. Imani drew this for me, with the perfect
scripture attached. She encourages me every day. The deepening of our friendship
is the greatest gift 2020 has given. I added words to her prayerful art.
Oh Lord, let me keep my morning eyes. ♥Kate

[18] Peterson, Eugene H. *The Message*. Colorado Springs, CO: NavPress, 2002. Print.

Morning Eyes

Kate

Sunrise on my porch
is beautiful besides
all that I bring with me,
when I come to sit in light.

The lift of sun cuts night,
as if it never were at all.
Sweet forgetfulness, stubborn hope,
too bright to hear the darkness call.

Like rays of sun I long to
reach, beyond night's deepest cries,
to shine, be damned despair!
Lord, help me keep my morning eyes.

Hide

Nancy

I want to hide,
Inside.
Here in my space.
At home where we're safe,
I can be blind.
Close my eyes
To what's real,
Put a limit on what I feel.
If we don't leave,
All we'll ever need
Is this home,
this shield.

I want to hide,
Inside.
Here in my space.
And believe we are OK.
I just want to be OK.

*"Trust in the Lord, and do good; dwell in the land and befriend faithfulness.
…Commit your way to the Lord; trust in him, and he will* ACT. *He will bring forth
your righteousness as the light, and your* justice *as the noonday. Be still before the Lord
and wait patiently for him; fret not yourself over the one who prospers in his way,
…Refrain from anger, and forsake wrath! Fret not yourself;
…those who wait for the Lord shall inherit the land.*
In just a little while, *…the meek shall inherit the land
and delight themselves in* abundant peace."

(*ESV*, Ps. 37.3, 5-11, emphasis added)[19]

Psalms

Mama

In just a little while…
wait just a memory more…
patient in your trial…
your meek beloved, though poor.
How I've been still!
How I've swallowed my shouts!
Hid in wings of your will;
persevered through my doubts.
But Lord! *How long?*
How long 'til our songs are sung?!
Lord! How long?
When does your promised inheritance come?
I don't know if I—
Lord?
—can stick to this weary, lonely path.
Do you still hear my cries?
Lord?
They've forsaken your name,
    I'm in shackles and shame,
        Son's not comin' home again…
           My Lord, where is your wrath?

---

[19] Study Bible-ESV. English Standard Version, Crossway Bibles, 2014.

Tell the Night

Shawna

Sitting at the table
running my hands
through my coily, curly hair,
I try to quiet my mind
of all the feelings
that slide down my throat
and settle near my breast.
Tightening my body,
I gird myself
tryna keep them out of my heart.
So, I tell the night
my troubles
and say the words I dare not say
for fear hatred will reside where forgiveness fitfully rests.

I intertwine my fingers
and in hushed tones
I tell the night
our pain.
Quietly, I spit out bitterness
so that even God can't hear
and rush to rescue my lips
with God's edict of pardon.
But before absolution,
I ask the night
"How long? How long do we wait?
How long do we march? How long do we pray?
How long do we forgive? How long do we cry?"

Sliding to my knees
I wait and listen.
The questions linger like shadows.
Hoping the night responds
to my interrogation,
I tell the night
the names of our lost ones,
whose guilt or innocence
was neither tried nor convicted
just covered in Black-ness.
But God heard
and sent Psalms
to soothe, comfort, and strengthen.
"Well played"
I tell the night.
"Well played."

Bombarded

Aliyah, Kate, Nancy

By news and noise.
By raised and silenced voice.
By ignorant, stubborn choice.
By memes made to annoy.
Bombarded.
By unexpected stills of joy.
By tears and fears that might destroy.
By precious strength left to deploy.
By hope saved if we will rejoice.
Bombarded.
Every.
Bombarded.
Single.
Bombarded.
Second.
Bombarded.

SHUT UP!

I Have Lost the Words

Imani

Words

I always have so many of them.
Waiting to be written and shaped,
Waiting to be sharpened and shaded,
Waiting to dust the page, painting in the light and dark places.
Waiting to tell the stories of the shadows and the hollows, as often as the mountain
tops.
But not now.

Now there is just waiting,

Without the words.

I keep looking around corners,
Hoping to see them.
Hoping to see people making choices I understand.
Hoping to see people loving people first.
Hoping to see the effects of stillness, for some, blossoming into beauty amidst
restlessness.
Hoping to see the appreciation of busyness, for others, blossoming into lasting
appreciation that becomes change.
Hoping to see a willingness to put others first, to see others, to sacrifice, because
life is valuable—every life.
But I don't.

Now there is just the hoping,

Without the seeing.

And I don't know what to say…

I have lost the words.

Or maybe I know where the words have gone,
But I cannot wield them now.
Because words have been reduced to gasoline, and opinions fire.
And this poet,
This artist,
This heart,
I cannot bear to watch any more of the world burn.

World War

Imani (Later around midnight,
the few, helpless words Imani found.)

The world is at war
with the war and the world.
We're tired of fighting,
yet fight more and more.
What's true we can't hear;
what we hear isn't true.
We mourn what we've lost,
just to lose what is new.

Flame

Kate

bone deep

pain

the press
the pull
the fire
of this ache
will not wane

though I trust
the voice
in my lungs
to speak truth
be it flames

it's lonely
to watch
ignorance
choose to dance
in cool waves

be they lies
borrowed time
lazy intellect
or brazen
disdain

they know not
the sheer cost
all that's lost
to commit
to be change

they know not
the sheer cost
to commit
to this

bone deep

pain

Peace Don't Know Me

Darius

Peace don't know me.
She don't know my name.
Never asked me my troubles.
Never tried to understand.
Just assigned more blame
For my circumstances.

Peace don't know me.
Walked by me and clutched
Her purse strings
Like I was trying to steal
What is rightly mine…
Justice and equality.

Peace don't know me.
Yet we coexist side by side.
Ignoring our failings to get along.
Shading beliefs
In an alternative reality,
Fighting
All my life.

Peace don't know me.
Never said my name.
Never felt my pain.
Yet saw me struggle,
Turned her back
And dared me to react.

Peace don't know me.
Though we are the same.
Saw my Blackness
And showed disdain
For my appeal to equity denied.
She never recognized my cries.

> *"Deep calls to deep at the roar of your waterfalls; all your breakers and your waves*
> *have gone over me. ...I say to God, my rock: 'Why have you forgotten me?*
> *Why do I go mourning because of the oppression of the enemy?'*
> *As with a deadly wound in my bones, my adversaries taunt me, while they say*
> *to me all the day long, 'Where is your God?' Why are you cast down,*
> *O my soul, and why are you in turmoil within me? Hope in God;*
> *for I shall again praise him, my salvation and my God."*

(*ESV*, Ps. 42.7, 9-11)[20]

In Deep

Imani

Chaos calls to chaos.
Deep calls out to deep.
Crashing, flooding, pressing,
these waters push down on me.
Sorrow rolls out to sorrow.
Troubles stack, again and again.
How do we reach your mountain of glory?
Without your help,
how do we swim?

How do we get there, Lord?
You are over the deep, the chaos.
Don't let us perish here, Lord!
Be deeper still, the deep who saves us.
Overpower and consume.
Purge like fire.
Please, renew.
Be deeper still
—the deep of you.

---

[20] Study Bible-ESV. English Standard Version, Crossway Bibles, 2014.

All the feels

Shawna

Faith and fear
Can't reside
In one place, so I hear.
Neither can peace and grace
Alongside sadness and pain
Reside in one place...
At least that's what they tell me.

But I feel all the feels...
Daily,
I falter in my attempt to be a blessing,
While being human.
Daily,
I inoculate myself and the world
With the Word.
On my knees
With hands lifted high,
Or fingers clinched
And head bowed,
Or lifted,
as I
Give thanks,
Ask for mercy,
Praise His name,
Pray for healing,
And *believe*
It is *done.*
Amen!

And then
...I still
Feel all the feels.
The very next day,
Until I kneel to pray.

Unsurprisable

Dr.

I shock
much less easily
than I did.
For shock and outrage
are the way
of the world.
The absurd and nonsensical
are so common
they're unremarkable.
Only sacrifice
and compromise
could surprise me
to hope in good.

Rain

Gretchen, Nancy, J.R., Aliyah, Darius

Gretchen

It's raining.
The air smells clean.
The grass is so green.
I'm invited in,

> **Nancy**
>
> to a cleansing,
> to growth,
> to permission
> to pause and feel both.

> **J.R.**
>
> The air is thick,
> and it presses,
> me down on this bench
> to sit,

> **Aliyah**
>
> to relish the sound
> of the water receding,
> carrying our fears
> and our smallness with it.

> **Darius**
>
> Maybe I'll rise.
> Maybe I'll hope again.
> Or maybe I'll be swept—
> to the place where the water ends.

Maybe I'll believe.

Maybe I'll gain.

Maybe I'll leave.

Maybe I'll stay.

Maybe I'll rain.

Hard

Gretchen

What is hard?
This.
Not this.

I have food.
Shelter.
Space.

I can't replace
the freedom
we lived.

But I can give
this stillness
grace.

I have guilt.
I am grateful.
I am worn.

Being still,
with plenty,
means I'm blessed.

But it's a test
to remember
this is freedom.

So many are dying,
so many crying,
their dreams torn.

We're playing games,
doing puzzles,
struggling with school.

Others are fighting
simply to breathe
on their own.

Nothing is known
except that all
is uncertain.

Behind hospital curtains,
behind these walls,
fear is cruel.

And none escape it.
Not in the suburbs.
Not in the cities.

Fear unites us.
The news incites us.
Anxiety equalizes.

As the sun rises
to a horror
on repeat.

Yet I am lucky.
Within these walls,
a safe retreat.

Sparks and Flares

Keep Praying

Darius (November 2, 2020, the night before the Presidential Election)

Mama, you keep saying to pray.
What has that done so far?
You keep getting on your knees,
Eyes closed
Not seeing what's happening to your people.
We are on our knees,
Hands up,
And still getting beaten.

Mama, you keep saying to pray.
That ain't done nothing so far.
Given a White Jesus
To keep us subservient,
To make us forgive this country while
We are on our knees,
Heads down,
And still getting mistreated.

Mama, you keep saying to pray.
Only time we're seen is on a video screen.
Or stomping in the streets
Demanding "No justice, no peace."
And justice is still absent.
We are on our knees.
Heads down,
Shackled into retreating.

Mama, you keep saying to pray.
Give me something else to do.
Give me something more powerful.
Give me a God that's for justice.
Give me a God that's for us.
Give me a God America will listen to.
Or maybe He doesn't hear my prayers, Mama.
Maybe America's prayers are louder, Mama.
Maybe the shouts that tell me to stand back and let God
Handle it and let God intervene
Pray harder than me, Mama.

Maybe for them, God has interceded
And chosen those proud boyz instead of you and me.

Mama, you keep saying to pray.
Please, Mama, tell me what to say.

Cried to the Lord

Mama (November 3, 2020, Election Day)

I cried to the Lord
"Help us, oh Lord"
Help us grieve and forgive
While we fight
The atrocities we receive.
Help us to maintain our humanity
In the face of indignity.
On bended knee
And with bowed head
I cried to the Lord
Deliver unto us a victory.

Polarized

Will

Polarized,
hypnotized
by fighting words
that criticize.
If we took
the time
to sympathize,
we just might
see light,
realize.
The cracks
in liberty
materialize,
the broken dreams
beneath the lies,
the rock,
the rubble
we justified,
its heartless truth
might come alive.

Instead,
we shout,
we theorize.
We cast our blame
to the other side.
We grossly
oversimplify,
with our memes,
our jeers,
we stigmatize.
My sisters,
brothers,
we're meant to rise!
Not some,
but ALL,
with one fell tide.

A tide we make,
fin'lly stand behind,
our promise to love
to equalize.

But are
those words
just empty cries?
Do we not
value
every life?
Too afraid
to open up
our eyes?
Instead,
content
to criticize,
with fighting words
to hypnotize.
To keep our land
not free,
not wise,
not brave,
not whole,
just polarized.

Stolen

J.R.

We will never give up,
Never concede.
You can't, when something's been stolen from under your feet.
The corrupt Left made sure they had the votes they needed.
We will keep fighting to the end.
And we won't accept Ka-Ma-La and Biden.
Only Trump can make America great again.

We will never give up,
Never concede.
Let's give the courts all the time they need.
Wait until they hear all the evidence.
It was a landslide victory, stolen from Trump and Pence.
We'll take our country back, there is no debate; we'll win.
Only Trump can make America great again!

Did You Fact Check That?

Dr.

Did you repost that?
The article with a catchy title
on your news feed
meant to mislead.
Did it succeed?
Were you an accomplice to stupidity?
Or just hypocrisy?
Did you fact check that?

Did a phrase for the agenda
you subscribe to
reflect Red or Blue?
Did your party loyalty cloud your intelligence?
What was in the sentence
that reeled you in
to a fallacy about democracy?
Did you fact check that?

Did you watch one news station
that demonized half the population?
That said the media (all but them) lie?
Were they far left or far right lies?
Were you surprised by the indoctrination
about fraudulent votes and a stolen election?
Did you fact check that?

Did you help bend the truth with opinion?
Did you do your due diligence
or just listen in?
Did a talking head convince you they were right?
Did it make you want to take up arms and fight?
What are you thinking?
Please, fact check that!

Ends Meet

Kate

We're making ends meet.
No sign of beginnings on our street,
but Jack's is once again open.
Will's still got a paycheck,
and that's something to hope in.

I saw Mama the other day.
Somehow that woman has strength to pray,
and her strength for me is catching.
Despite my tears, despite my anger,
her choice to kneel is course-correcting.

So, we're making ends meet.
No sign of beginnings on our street,

but we'll keep making ends meet.
We'll keep making the ends meet.

On My Block

Ty

Lately there's been no hashtags
To tell you about the struggle.
So, you forgot.
No one organized a march.
No protests erupted.
No one shouted Blue Lives Matter
To drown out the cries that Black Lives Matter.
No Black Lives were silenced by a Blue badge held by a White hand;
Or so you think.

On my block
Sirens blared.
Red and blue lights spun into view
And I assumed the position
Like my daddy taught.
No sudden moves, pull to a well-lit spot,
Don't need no shadows to block the view.
Place hands at 10 and 2.
And be sure not to move.
My eyes trained forward
On the road and I didn't dare
Stare.
You saw no hashtags or videos so,
You didn't think about the deaths today.
Brown or Black,
Guilty or innocent,
Tried or executed.

On my block
It was business as usual.
We voted, those who could.
We prayed, those who would.
Still shift into fear
At the sound of sirens.
Still got our hands at 10 and 2.
Still dare not move.

But now, we look at the officer's eyes.
And some even ask "why?"
Head held high with pride,
Others seething with anger.
Both dancing with danger,
Thankful for those hashtags and videos
Showing what could happen, guilty or not
On my block.

Fits the Description

Hate

He was 6ft 2
Black hoodie and tennis shoes.
No, he was 5ft 10
Blue sweatshirt and steel toed boots.
No, I swear I saw him
As clear as day.
He was 185lbs and he went that way.
No, Sir. He was right in front of me
And I'll never forget,
He was 200 lbs, 6ft and he was wearing red.
He had short hair,
No, it was long.
Yeah, that's what I said.
He was wearing a baseball cap and his hair was in dreads.
He was running.
No, he was walking, and he kept looking back.
Yeah, I know what he looks like.
And I can't forget it,
He fits the description—
He was Black.

No More

Will

I cannot take another conspiracy theory.
My soul is tired. My understanding strained.
I've taken to snoozing people I love,
because I cannot read their memes.
This level of exhaustion and fatigue
is more than Kate and I can bear.
We have our children, we have our work,
we have 2020-induced relational tears.
"No, we're not coming to Thanksgiving."
"Yes, we will miss you, but it's not safe."
"Yes, we support #blacklivesmatter."
"No, voting for Biden is not killing babies."
So, please, forgive me, if for this moment,
I must take a holiday from the noise.
I still want to be a voice of reason.
But for now, I must quiet your voice.

No Vaccine

Dr.

There's no vaccine for hate.
If I've learned anything,
you wouldn't take it.
There's no vaccine that can bring change.
If I've learned anything,
you would change it.
So, what's the best that we can do?
Play percentages and odds?
Build up immunity for a few,
and leave the rest of you to God?

Faith Not Fear[21]

Imani (December 14, 2020)

I have faith.
I have fears.
I might not need my faith without them.
I have faith.
I have doubts.
Though you have a faith I'm not allowed in.
How does that work?
All White, no gray?
How can your faith
deny my facts?
So little space,
yet much to say.
Too much science
and your faith cracks?

But I suppose
I'm not surprised.
Covid is only the latest attack.
You have your world
erected just right.
There's no room for gray *and* no room for Black.
When I speak what's truth,
you call it dramatic.
A world that is White,
you just call pragmatic.
So little space,
yet so much to say.
Is it fear that you fear
to make ignorance faith?

---

[21] While daily deaths from Covid continue making history everyday as "deadliest days," each of these poems reference a familiar battle cry of anti-maskers: "Faith not Fear."

Faith Not Fear?

Nancy

My sister is sick.
My baby sister.
She was given
Remdesivir today.
Her oxygen's 80.
And it's not climbing.
All of my friends
tell me they'll pray.
My same friends
who went into Walmart,
no mask
or just using their shirt.
My same friends
who hosted Thanksgiving,
no mask
who now say they love her.

They tell me, "Have faith.
Not fear."
But I no longer know
what they mean.
My sister had faith.
Not fear.
And now my sister
struggles to breathe.
Who is this faith
really in?
It seems that God
is using her doctors,
who use a science
that God has made.
And our "fearless" faith?

    …just makes us imposters.

Complicated Friendship

Kate, Darius

Kate

I'll always pray for you.
I've known you all my life.
My brother from another mother,
My neighbor.
I'll raise my voice
Above the shouting, above the noise,
To protect you,
And advocate for you
When they demonize you,
Bind you,
Reject you,
Deny you your rights,
Freedom and humanity,
Justice and life.
Whether I'm marching in the streets
Painted with your blood and tears
Until there is no more blood and tears.
Whether you are saints or sinners
With skin black as night or with just a drop-
That one made up rule-
Along with all the others,
To label you
Different and
Dangerous
When you are clearly both and neither...
Complicated is our friendship.

Darius

Complicated is our friendship
As I am labeled with "the others".
At least outwardly, by history.
But what we share is bigger than the outside noise.
We are family.
I will always pray for you, too,
Just like I know you pray for me.
Standing on two separate islands
We can fill the void left by the separateness
Of our factions.
I'll shout above the noise
To defend you
And endorse you
When they label you
Privileged,
When they blame you
For the skin you're in,
Or because you defend
Me, when they raised you
Different.
Ours is a complicated friendship.

Essential Now

Ty

I deliver your packages.
I smile.
You smile back.
You liar.
I'm essential now,
deliverin' Christmas.
With my back,
fullfillin' your wishes.
But tomorrow
is my day off.
And no, I don't like
to be out in this khaki.
I ain't your boy,
and I'm no man's lackey,
but I'll be masked up
because I ain't tacky.
I'll do my shoppin',
just like you.
Ain't found for my mama
yet all she's due.
And maybe out there,
I'll pass you by.
It's happened before,
though you never say hi.
I see you daily,
but you don't see me.
Because out on the streets,
You ain't ever smiled at me.
I deliver your packages.
I smile.
You smile back.
You liar.

Young Man

Nancy

There's a boy who delivers my packages,
Fine, good lookin' young man.
He does his job with pride and politeness,
Freely giving "yes sirs" and "yes ma'ams."

I've been watching him a little more lately,
Wondering who he is off my street.
He works hard, looks smart in his uniform.
Isn't he what a Black man should be?

I'm not sure if that's a thought I should have.
I'm not sure anymore what is right.
Though I see him most days, I've not
once asked him his name.
Would I know it
          ...if he were White?

If the news showed his face, empty hands,
and arms raised,
would I question
          ...if it was right?

Well

Shawna (December 24, 2020, Christmas Eve)

Our bodies are well,
PPE in place,
my people OK.
At least physically.
There's little to do for the rest
but pray.
I'm bone deep tired.
It's harder and harder
each day to smile.
If there was a time, I needed Jack,
it is now.

Yet he's still gone.
So, I get up.
I go to work,
and I come home.
And I get up.
I go to work.
Then I'm alone.

It Isn't Christmas

Gretchen (December 25, 2020, Christmas Day)

It isn't Christmas.
Not really.

It's quarantined
To be seen
By family.
It's same ol' tidings
World still fighting
Calamity.
It's too hard believing
Hate's still tweeting
Insanity.
Even for auld lang syne
Can't turn my eye
From this tragedy.

It isn't Christmas.
Not really.

While Black

Darius, Imani, Ty, Aliyah, Shawna, Sisters, Brothers (December 26, 2020)

The deaths are still going.
Blood and tears are still flowing
Even if you don't see it anymore.
Even when the hashtags and the marches
Cease to stream on your nightly news
Begging for views
And reviews
Of those confused
About why we still march,
Why we still kneel,
Why we still carry our phones
To document the plight
And the fight
For our visibility
To be decriminalized
For our existence to be humanized.
To eat in peace,
Walk in silence
Wear a hoodie,
Drive,
Shop, go to school
Fail and succeed
While Black.

Living while Black is still going.
It's still happening without video.
Your acknowledgement
Occurs when it's convenient
And cool,
Trending on your feed,
A meme you can repost
About a march or a video
Or a book to be…woke.
While you cradle
Biases held near your breast,
Housed in your thoughts,
And built into the systems,
Judicial, financial, and social

Which still dwell in the beliefs you deny
Even to your "Black friends."
Persistently consistent
in blissful, complicit ignorance
to what it means
to be living
While Black.

Windows

Gretchen

There's a light that shines in through my every window.
It's been there since the day I was born.
I've assumed that every other soul must have one.
I've never questioned that the light is mine to own.

But lately I've been prone to ask more questions.
I've gone to wander streets with windows often dark.
In these places privileged light, left, deserted,
I've heard stories that when told create a spark.

These windows do not need me to bring my spotlight—
to turn it on and be some hero of the day.
No, there are heroes living here behind dark windows.
They have the power within their voices to light up streets, hearts, and change.

Yet for me, there is still something left to do here.
And it isn't to slink in silence to easy light.
I can recognize, first, I did nothing to turn my light on.
Then I can listen with open ears, an open mind, and open eyes.

Yes, I can lean into the truth hushed within these shadows.
Peer in windows I might otherwise have never seen.
And I can end this lighted cycle of preserving my own comfort.
Because a legacy of lighted windows cost a darkness I *can't* unsee.

Spark

Imani

Soon

Nancy

Soon
it will be
time to plant
things
in pots
hanging dead
now.

Soon
it will be
time to grow
dreams
in soil
hanging cold
now.

Soon
it will be
time to bloom
spring
in our lives
standing still
now.

Soon
it will be
time to know
me
standing new
in what I choose
now.

A Year Like No Other

Gretchen

All the things I've let go,
All the things I did not know
I could lose.
And what's new I've made grow,
All the things I did not know
I could choose.

What's left is true and its mine.
All the things I've walked through
I won't be blind.
Imperfect and cold, imperfect and right,
All the things I've walked through
have sharpened my sight.

On this other side, will I know you? Your name
On the lips of my memory
But not unchanged.
On this other side will you know me? My name
On the lips of your memory
But not unchanged.

So, what happens next, now,
In this quiet? What happens next, how,
In this noise?
Who will we be next, now,
in this breaking? In this building who, now,
hears our voice?

All the things we've let go,
All the things we did not know
We could lose.
All that's new we've made grow,
All the things we did not know
We could choose…

Top

Imani

> I'm starting to believe that hope is active.
> You only need the mountain top to be real,
> when you are pushing a rock uphill.

Embody

Brothers

Won't embody the lies—you speak
About my people—about me.
Won't stop pursuing the justice—I seek
For folks who look—like me.
I'm taking the lead—finally.
And standing on my feet—firmly.
No more kneeling—for me.
I'm marching, speaking out, protesting—I'm free.
Organizing, voting—democracy.
Tired of forgiving and forgetting—that's weak.
Standing firm, rising up—I'll speak.
Advocating, educating—for me.
Building my community—strictly.
Challenging stereotypes you push—weary.
Embodying words my mama prayed—over me.
Role model, smart, loved—kingly.
Hands at 2 and 10—so I live to see
My son grow up proud—Black like me.
Embody.

234

Enough

Shawna (for her children)

"Am I enough?"
I hate that you'll ask.
But you will.
"Am I really enough?"
It's a lurking, persistent question,
and no one avoids it.
It's powerful;
it's powerless.
It all depends on what you hear.
Do you hear the echo
of doubt
planted and sown?
Or do you hear a challenge,
an opportunity
to get up yet again.
A chance to leave the
naysayers and custodians of
powerless, fearful questions.
To be swept up
in forward motion,
brave enough to own your story.
Because *you*
were always
enough.

Tangled Clarity

Gretchen (On Sunday morning)

In my tangled clarity
I see you there,
But I cannot stop.
No space to explain.
We've made our choices.
So very different.
And talking about us
Won't make us change.
It's tangled clarity
Because I feel,
Because you feel,
Because much hurts.
But in that jumble,
There's been a grounding.
I know my own knots;
They don't need to be yours.
They can't be yours;
They aren't yours.

Kate (On Sunday morning)

In my tangled clarity
I see the big picture,
With some details fuzzy.
But the feelings are clear, sharp,
Piercing through reality.
We've made our choices.
So very different.
Each of us
Steadfast in our beliefs.
Unyielding in our views.
Our opposition
Won't let us change
Our tangled clarity,
These tangled days.

Blossoms

Kate

As a child,
Stephen Crane taught me
that youthful innocence,
beauty—*life*—
can "[blossom]
in a mud puddle,"
even if the dark,
one day,
folds hopes
back into mud.

Standing in my kitchen, now,
I unwrapped
a piece of chocolate,
and a promise
written within
reminded me of
Stephen's Maggie.
Here,
in this mud puddle,
"cherish the blossoms."

What can we grow
within this fear,
this soil of death,
this mud of tears?
What might live
to shock with bloom,
daring youthful spirit
us consume?
And can we hold back the dark
of mud that will still come?

I do not know.
I cannot see.

But I won't let
my heart believe
that every Maggie
of the street
blooms only once
for few to see.
No, I will water,
I will cherish *every* seed.

Let not the innocence
and the light
become just echoes
in this night.
Yes, when beauty, yes, when life,
dares to blossom in this strife,
on the edge, of this knife—
blooming wild, free, and right—
for these blossoms, in this mud,
we must *fight*.[22]

---

[22] The quotation, "[blossom] in a mud puddle," is from Chapter V of Stephen Crane's, *Maggie: A Girl of the Streets* (Crane, Stephen. *Maggie: A Girl of the Streets and Other Short Fiction.* Bantam Books, 1986.). The quotation "cherish the blossoms" is from a dark chocolate Dove Promise, circa Christmas 2020 ;).

Echo

Mama, Aliyah (December 31, 2020, New Year's Eve)

Mama	**Aliyah**

Mama

The echo of pain
The echo of same
The echo of nothing changed.

Aliyah

The soft beat of hope
As marching feet know
From shaken ground nothing may grow.

The echo of Sons
The echo of love
The echo of what was once.

Our tears of resilience
A spotlight in stillness
Yet still we have no deliverance.

The echo of pain
The echo of same
The echo of nothing changed.

May our cries pierce your night
May our blood stain your eyes
May your *change* finally dawn in our skies.

The Longest Year

Kate (December 31, 2020, New Year's Eve)

In **January**—
I had dreams,
I had resolutions;
For tiny problems,
I even had solutions.

> In **February**—
> I had our lives,
> I had no way to know,
> that come March
> I would have to let them go.

> In **March**—
> I had words,
> I had space;
> I had fears and uncertainty
> For these unprecedented days.

In **April**—
I had to adjust,
I had fatigue;
I had a wanderer's
Unmet need to leave.

> On **May 25th**—
> I had shock,
> No more air;
> I had disbelief
> That we lost George Floyd there.

May's final days—
I had disgust,
I had pause.
How could people I love,
Not take up this cause?

By **June**—
I had rage,
I had conviction;
Crying their names,
Too many untold victims.

Come **July**—
I had sorrow,
I had resignation;
Even a plague
Could not awaken our selfish nation.

In **August**—
I had trepidation,
I had hard decisions.
How could choosing caution
Ever cause such wide divisions?

In **September**—
I had no space,
I had no words;
I had virtual school,
Long hours, tears, and hurts.

By **October**—
I had exhaustion,
I had my early vote;
I had to trust
Humanity had taken notes.

In **November**—
I had relief,
I had sobering truth;
We were still divided,
But small hope had taken root.

This **December**—
I had Christmas,
I had quiet;
I turned off the world
Looking inward with calm defiance.

Now **Christmas** is past—
January looms,
I have clarity.
I have no misconceptions
About the depths of our disparity.

In **2021**—
Will I have change?
Will we rediscover humanity?
Is God's grace big enough
To return our civility?

For **now**—
I have my hope,
I have my doubt;
But this selfish independence,
Can no longer be what we're about.

Gasoline

Fear

Hate (January 1, 2021)

Who am I,
if I'm not better?
Who am I,
if I'm not taller,
not stronger?
Who am I,
if I'm not more worthy?
Who am I,
if I'm not richer,
not smarter?
Who am I,
if the natural order's unnatural?
Who am I,
if this was power,
not providence?
Who am I,
if I'm not an heir to this land?
Who am I,
if we were never fair,
not sovereign?
Who am I,
if I'm not better—
        though Whiter—
                than Black?

Outskirts

Brothers

Pushed to the
Outskirts
Of justice,
Of fairness,
Of representation.
How are we to react
To all that's happening around us?
Marching in the streets,
Mistrust of the systems in place
For hundreds of years.
They don't represent us anymore;
Or did they ever?
Ignored.

Living on the
Outskirts,
You didn't see us until
We yelled, rioted, pushed against the barricades,
And demanded what's rightly ours.
Birthright, American rights,
Civil Rights.
Your ivory tower has to come down.
Fists up, signs high.
While you sit in seats we put you in.
Pushing us out.
Ignored.

Not today!
Today we push back.
March, protest, demonstrate
Our power to disrupt
The corrupt.
Democracy, be my friend.
We challenge you to do what
Needs to be done, what's never been done.
Tired of the outskirts,
We are pushing in, taking up space.
You can't ignore us.

J.R.

Pushed to the
Outskirts
By liberals,
By media,
By affirmative action.
How are we to react
When our way of life is being stolen?
Marching in the streets,
Mistrust of the powers rising,
Destroying hundreds of years.
Will they represent us anymore?
Loyal Patriots!
Now ignored.

Living as the
Silenced,
You didn't listen until
We yelled, rioted, pushed against the barricades,
And demanded what's rightly ours.
Birthright, American rights,
Conservative Rights.
Your rise to power has to fall.
Guns up, signs high.
While you sit in seats lies put you in.
Pushing us out.
Ignored.

Not today!
Today we push back.
March, protest, demonstrate
Our power to disrupt
The corrupt.
Fringes, be my friend.
We challenge you to do what
Needs to be done, preserve the way it's done.
Tired of the outskirts,
We are pushing in, taking back space.
You can't ignore us.

Who Is Responsible?

Mama

When fires are lit,
Who is responsible?

If the flame licks at your door
But does not burn?
If the glow lights up the night,
Melting fear and bringing warmth
That disturbs
all that's quiet, safe and dark, small and yours?
Who is responsible?

If the flame is lit indoors
not tamed and driven wild?
If anger shatters glass and walls,
Destroying sacredness for miles?
If oppression, hate, and fear
Litter matches, washed in tears?
Who is responsible?

If your power incites flame
Stealing peace, if justice burns?
If you sit back, and watch it claim
Lives and dreams, while wielding words?
If from chaos houses fall,
If over ash your footsteps trod?
Who is responsible?

When fires are lit,
Who is responsible?

Did You See?

Ty (January 6, 2021)

Turn on the news!
Did you see this shit?
What the hell is going on?
This is crazy!
They pushed and shoved to make their way in.
Where are the National Guards for them?
Where are the batons and the tear gas for them?
Where are the handcuffs and arrests for them?
How did the Confederate flag
Cast a shadow on the Capitol steps
And inside those hallowed halls?
How did a police shield become an instrument to break windows?
How were some officers overwhelmed by the crowd,
While others stepped aside to take selfies with the demonstrators?
How the hell did they get to be named demonstrators?
If it had been Black Lives how many would be dead?
How many would have mug shots
And be labeled thugs by the president or coworkers?

I Saw It.

Darius (January 6, 2021)

Man, I saw that shit,
I am, and I'm not surprised.
We don't even get close enough to show the whites of our eyes.
Civil Rights are different from refusing to accept an election defeat.
But to hear them tell it, they're righteous, unlike you and me.
They claim to be marginalized and invisible, unseen by the government.
When we claim inequality and injustice, it's labeled entitlement.
Justice denied is justice to no one.
It's unbelievable that the Capitol was overrun.
Smashed windows and lifted signs,
While congressional representatives sheltered inside.
The hypocrisy of this "demonstration" demands to be reckoned with.
Even though I saw it, I still can't believe this shit.

The President of the United States

Hate (January 6, 2020, Trump's video for those attempting a coup at the Capitol.)

"I know your pain.
I know you're hurt.
We had an election that was stolen from us.
It was a landslide election,
and everyone knows it,
especially the other side.
But you have to go home now.
We have to have peace.
We have to have law and order.
We have to respect our great people in law and order.
We don't want anybody hurt.
It's a very tough period of time.
There's never been a time like this
where such a thing happened
where they could take it away from all of us.
From me,
from you,
from our country.
This was a fraudulent election
but we can't play into the hands
of these people.
We have to have peace.
So go home.
We love you.
You're very special.
You've seen what happens.
You see the way others are treated
that are so bad
and so evil.
I know how you feel.
But go home
and go home in peace."[23]

---

[23] A full transcription of President Donald Trump's words from a video he released on social media hours after the capital was overrun. Because President Trump's social media accounts have been suspended as of the time of publication of this book (or content has been removed/taken-down by social media companies because of the content's potential to incite further violence) it was difficult to find the video again for citation purposes. Consequently, we cannot guarantee that the link we provide will remain available. (*See* C-SPAN. "President Trump Video Statement on Capitol Protesters."

No. Full Stop.

Darius

I am not "these people."
I am We, the people.
You do not "love" me,
and I'd agree that we're not equal.
For you are lawless:
A tyrant who never loved this land.
You just love power.
So against you, we'll take our stand.

Evil

Imani

Evil isn't one man,
the head of the snake.
The body makes the head stand,
high in its place.
It's easy to call the eyes evil,
condemn the forked tongue.
But what of the masses of people,
who give rise to the one?

Are they neither good nor bad,
but just human like clay,
pliable and susceptible
to become the body of the snake?
The insecurities that lead to slithering,
the need for power and inclusion,
lead "the chosen" to enact their withering:
Trading goodness for sweet delusion.

C-SPAN, c-span.org, 6 Jan. 2021, https://www.c-span.org/video/?507774-1/president-trump-claims-election-stolen-tells-protesters-leave-capitol. Accessed 13 Mar. 2021.)

No Spin

Aliyah

Stop saying "protest."
Fools boots are on Pelosi's desk.
These are terrorists.
Do not call them something less.
This was a coup.
I will not hear your lame excuse.
They shamed the red, white, and the blue,
your president said, "We love you."
Are you kidding me?
You've lost all of your integrity.
Crying "Antifa" is solidarity
meant to disguise their white supremacy.
Well we won't have it!
You will not win, we will not quiet.
We will build back, where you divide us;
we will vote change and unite us,
for this is appalling!
A woman died for their stonewalling[24],
but her blood is not now calling
for democracy's overhauling.
Because "enough
is enough is enough!"[25]
This isn't tough.
This isn't sacrifice, or righteous rebuff,
a bully's militia in need of handcuffs.
For this was sedition.
Don't lay down tracks, a new rendition.
You cannot spin this with revisions,
hide your hate in supposition.

---

[24] Initial reports noted only one casualty as a result of the attack on the Capitol. When everything was over, there would be five names counted among the dead.

[25] President Elect Joseph Biden's words in a televised speech, on January 6, 2021, calling President Trump to make an official statement condemning the violence at the Capitol. (@CBSthismorning. "After his speech, President-elect Biden was asked if he was concerned about the safety of his inauguration, Biden said: 'I am not concerned. The American people are going to stand up and stand up now. Enough is enough, is enough.'" *Twitter*, 6 Jan. 2021, 3:20 pm, https://twitter.com/cbsthismorning/status/1346929610777382914?s=21.)

Such racist fear!
When your false king called them here,
they grabbed the wheel, thought they could steer
because they're "special" to the puppeteer?
Well they're not Vikings.
And dude, that hat, it isn't striking.[26]
This is AMERICA, and you're done whining.
Ratify that vote, 'cause we're done hiding.

[26] A tattooed, shirtless man, wearing a horned Viking hat and covered in red, white, and blue face and body paint became a familiar image when mobs stormed the Capitol. The man, a 32-year-old Trump supporter and conspiracy theorist, had previously become a familiar face at pro-Trump-rallies. He is also known to have counter-protested at Black Lives Matter rallies.

Bullshit

Ty[27]

They stood on the capitol steps
with guns we could never hold.
They refused to wear the masks
that protect their neighbor, young and old.
That protect me. That protect my mama,
that protect grandmas. Mine and theirs.
Would they ever riot for my rights??
Fuck no, for Black men they don't care.
Well, FUCK them! I won't be silenced!
Maybe this plague will wipe them out.
For all their evangelical BULLSHIT,
there ain't no love in what they shout.
So, let them go on, show their asses,
over a freedom they already have.
They ain't ever known chains
        Because they make chains.
Go on maskless fuckers,
        breathe the air that you've made bad.

---

[27] Written in the spring, **early May**, right after White rioters tried to take the Michigan capitol. All these months, all this time, all these voices raised, so many died, and Ty recalls how nothing has changed. Another Capitol stormed and lives taken.

There Are No Winners

Shawna

Unprepared and overrun.
Officers scrambled to protect and serve.
It's what they meant to do.
Politics be damned,
As opposite sides huddled together
Forgetting red and blue,
Left and Right.
Shocked by glass breaking
As splinters of
Fear, anger, disillusionment, and entitlement
Pierced the seat of legislation.
There are no winners here.

Amped up and incited by a careless leader
Too focused on self
To secure democracy,
A crowd, eager to stomp on righteousness,
Fueled by hate and fed by lies,
Soiled an American legacy.
Ensconced in a web of lies and denial,
They were sent to disrupt
A nation.
And they did.
There are no winners here.

There are no winners here.
No one, not one Republican, Democrat, or Independent
Is the victor.
We, the American people,
All lost today.
Lost the belief that our votes,
No matter the outcome,
Would be respected,
Protected.
There are no winners here.

The breach, like that of an ill designed levee,
Allowed the flow of homegrown violence
To flood the halls leaving debris
Of disbelief that our very foundation
Could be shattered by a fraud
Using small words,
Catering to small minds,
With a big intent
To stop the counting of votes.
There are no winners here.

America, we've revealed our cracks
To the world.
We've shown them
We care more about political parties
Than what's just.
We are so divided
That democracy has been put in a corner,
Shielded by an overwhelmed security force.
Forced to fight, retreat,
Or worse,
Choose their allegiance
To political party and personal preference over duty to country.
There are no winners here.

Are You the Only Ones?

Darius

Why is it OK
For you to carry guns?
Police stand back,
Don't attack,
Are you the only ones?
Responsible enough
We should trust
Your sons?
Your protests
Are demonstrations,
The rioting's only us?

Why is it OK
For you to break down doors?
Smash glass,
Attack,
Is that what liberty is for?
Are you the only ones
Can put Jesus on your signs?
Those outside
Do no harm,
Those out of hand
A different kind?

Why is it OK
For you to judge democracy,
Commit atrocities
And you're patriots,
Yet we're just lootin' thugs?
Are you the only ones
Can get angry
And stay righteous,
Murderin' cops
Who don't stand back?
Yeah, you're the only ones.

HOWEVER

Kate, J.R. (January 7, 2021)

Kate   **J.R.**

More shocking than yesterday's insurrection
Is today's justifications and protections,

> "No, they shouldn't have stormed those steps,
> HOWEVER, we can't ignore the threats
> of liberal lies and media deceptions."

Can my ears be hearing you correctly?
Are you defending terrorism indirectly?

> "Sure, some folks went a little too far,
> HOWEVER, we know Anitifa was at the heart.
> Too long good people have been disrespected."

HOWEVER, democracy has spoken!
HOWEVER, your patriotism is broken!
How dare you believe it is your right
to hold the power or else you'll fight?
How dare you desecrate those halls!
Imperfect system, still hallowed walls?
HOWEVER, the Capitol is not your ground!
HOWEVER, do NOT "Stand by"[28] Stand down!
How dare you bristle to be called privileged,
soaked in Trumpism's religion?
Will not relinquish even inches.
How dare you proclaim that this is Christian!
My Jesus laid down his life!
My Jesus believed in sacrifice!
You believe in sacrificing others,
Black bodies stolen from screaming mothers.

> "No this wasn't like blacklivesmatter,
> They are Marxist, but we're not facsist!
> We're simply taking back the castle."

---

[28] *See* footnote 17.

(Kate)   **(J.R.)**

HOWEVER, we do NOT have a King!
HOWEVER, you are NOT a majority!
And you have never known true silence.
Never shackled. Always defiant.

                    "Hard working people,"

yet so reliant
on unequal systems that now you riot?
For your pride, for first fruits,
for the way it's been, for racist roots.

                    "Now come on, you're getting loud,
                    all worked up, like that liberal crowd,
                    HOWEVER, if we don't act now
                         …we will still be around?"

No.

Because to tyranny, to white supremacy,
we will not bow.

Fire in a Crowded Theater

Will

How can you defend the actions of an unfit fanatic?
Inflammatory words,
Like swords viciously slicing through democracy,
Emboldened a crowd of puppets
Whose strings were tightly wound
To purposely assault the process of a nation.
He yelled
"Fire" in a crowded theater!
Simultaneously prodding supporters into illegal actions,
Briefly paralyzing the legitimate transfer of power,
And scorching the stripes on the flag.
Indefensible.

Unpresidential

Dr.

Tweedle dee, Tweedle dumb,
Two fingers and two thumbs
Played to the least of us,
Sparked the anger in us.
Black and White sticks,
Republican and Democratic,
Rubbed together to torch
Our country.
The Narcissist blamed and smiled,
Goaded and separated us—
Our Americanism vs White Nationalism.
Left and Right,
Red, white, & blue tinged with
Unpresidential and unfounded claims of fraud
That scattered doubt and
Picked at the scabs
Unhealed for generations.
An Uncivil War,
Raging on Facebook and Twitter.
As you pander to the Boyz,
Those you called "patriots"
And "very good people,"
More loyal to you than to truth,
common sense,
Or common justice.
Wanting it all for themselves.
How unpresidential
To pour doubt on the press
Who press you for answers,
The truth.
Tiny fingers spreading big lies,
Big enough to burn
The stitches of a frayed tapestry,
Pieced together by our differences
but held together by our dreams
Of America, practical or not.
Your job, Sir,
Is to hold it together,

But you are so
Unpresidential.[29]

---

[29] Donald Trump has used the term "patriots" to describe his supporters many times, but he did it again on Jan. 8, 2021, just two days after those same supporters attacked and occupied the Capitol Building (Meredith Corporation. "Hours After Telling Followers Who Rioted They're Un-American, Trump Calls Supporters 'Patriots': President Donald Trump also tweeted that he would not be attending Joe Biden's inauguration this month." *People*, People.com, 8 Jan. 2021,
https://www.google.com/amp/s/people.com/politics/less-than-two-days-after-deadly-capitol-mob-trump-calls-his-supporters-patriots/%3famp=true. Accessed 8 Jan. 2021.).

Just months before the Capitol attack, Trump referred to armed anti-maskers and Trump supporters who occupied the Michigan Capitol Building as "very good people" (Ecarma, Caleb. "Of Course Trump Called Armed, Right-Wing Protesters 'Very Good People.'" *Vanity Fair*, Vanityfair.com, 1 May 2020, https://www.google.com/amp/s/www.vanityfair.com/news/2020/05/donald-trump-called-armed-right-wing-protesters-good-people/amp. Accessed 8 Jan. 2021.).

It's Hard to Tell

Shawna

Marching through the streets,
Feeling marginalized.
Fighting for their rights,
Homemade and printed signs.
Make America great again
Or support Black Lives.
Banners swaying
To the rhythm of the masses
Of Black and White faces
Demanding justice—
For hashtags buried by Blue Lives
And citizens who feel cast aside.
Civil disobedience
Wafting through the crowd
Like a contact high.
Strangers inhaling the feeling
Of too much and enough
Start to rattle the streets.

Who are the bad guys?
It's hard to tell when they became enemies,
Or if they always were
Just because.

In uniform,
Suited and booted,
Today, willfully step aside.
Shields and batons
All at the ready,
Tear gas on standby.
If they get out of order,
Keep them at bay
And hold them back.
Crush the uprising
Stand firm, stand tall.
Don't let them through.
No, not one.
But these, let them have a free for all.

Maybe, just maybe let them have their way.
Black Lives flags will never pass,
But the Confederate gets to stay.
Be stoic in your appearance,
Don't let them see you sweat.
Smile, take pictures with them,
These, they're as American as you can get.
Don't let them through.
Don't let them get any closer.
Beat them where they stand;
Because they are anti-police and anti-American.

Who are the bad guys?
It's hard to tell when they became enemies,
Or if they always were
Just because.

If Not Now, When?

Silent Right, Aliyah

Silent Right

Stop fighting and inciting.
Everyone take a step back and relax.
You cannot change the world with words.
Only Word made flesh can do that.

But above all else protect *our* freedom,
First Amendment speech more precious than gold.
If *we* can't unleash our fighting words,
all that is good will be destroyed.

                Aliyah

                Where is there power?
                When is *my* voice a method of change?
                When do my words matter?
                When can conviction take up space?

                If not now, when?
                When the torches are at my door?
                Can I speak then?
                When we've lost everything worth fighting for?

                If not now *when?*

Shame on You

J.R., Darius, Nancy

J.R.

Shame on you
supporting the vote
of a stolen election,
room full of turncoats.
And Pence at the helm!
Rides the fence like a whelp,
as his House of cowards
let our voices sunset.
Good riddance, goodbye!
Raised your white flags to lies,
so we'll cast you aside.
Trump doesn't need your help.
With the first two amendments,
you ain't even defendin',
we'll march on these streets
'till the whole world is listenin'!
We'll do what we must
to preserve what is good,
what's righteous and true,
the real red, white and blue.
We'll keep our fine President!
Our majority will silence,
for once and for all,
this Leftist defiance.

Darius

Shame on you
with your violence,
suppressing our vote,
too afraid to let your tyranny go.
Shouting fraud like its fact
doesn't make it more true.
With the way that you act,
who should listen to you?
Stealing podiums,
smashing windows,
dragging men down the steps.
I saw the Oval defend you
beating officers to death.
Your President isn't mine.
No, he can't represent me.
He may love you, but I—
I will love democracy!
January the twentieth
couldn't come fast enough.
You say you'll bring civil war,
with your hate and your guns,
but you will not succeed,
no matter how much you burn.
Wake up! This is the end of hate's term.

Nancy

Shame on you
with your tweets
and your Parler retreats.
Defending insurgence
with your right to speak.
I may not like censure
as much as the next,
but I will not support
Trump inciting this death.
Five dead! Many injured,
my stomach in knots.
The hate they were shouting,
I've heard in your mouths.
Hell, I've heard it in mine,
I'm ashamed to admit,
but this is too far,
and they tried to lynch Pence?!
I'm done with it all!
I can't see a good side,
but I'm sad on this day
to admit I've no pride
for the idol I've made
of the Republican party.
From grace, it is clear,
we've fallen away.

Heal, You Say

Shawna

Heal, you say?
How can we, after today?
Calling for prayer, healing, and unity
Is impossible without equity and accountability.
A violent insurrection incited by a man you pledge to follow.
My friend, your call for unity is dismissive and hollow.
Getting back to normal would be comforting to you.
Eyes wide shut, ears closed, and denying what's true.
From day one his words, you won't denounce!
Their actions, you excuse, not renounce.
Blissfully ignorant, you claim to have been,
But the crisis in this country can't be unheard nor unseen.
Excuses be damned and erased.
Such loyalty for a man or political party is misplaced.

Yet you call for prayer and God's will to be done.
Call for Trump to be done! For them, those subversives, to be done.
What has occurred in our country, in our Capitol, in our House, cannot be undone.
My friend, without justice and reform no healing can begin.
Without acknowledging
Wrong doing,
wrong thinking,
wrong supporting,
There can be no unity
Without accountability!
Ostrich people with your head in the sand,
This country, nor this flag can withstand
Your kind of *ignor*-ance. How wrong
This passive prayer to let go and let God—we've heard far too long
And played along.
It wasn't easy but that's how it was done.
Praying for peace, marching for justice,
Hoping for healing and simmering in silence.

Heal, you say?

Officer[30]

Mama

Some now sit in judgment of your badge.
Some question who you serve
And if your personal beliefs
Become the shield you use
Against laws you swore to uphold.
Not me, not today.
You gave your life,
Protecting those you both agree with and not.
Standing up to those told to
Stand back and standby.
As doors crashed under the pressure of entitlement and insurgency,
You shielded our representatives
As they lifted democracy on their shoulders.
Your family lost you
Senselessly.
And for you,
we all grieve,
For you, we pray.

---

[30] Brian Sicknick, a Capitol police officer, was killed by insurgents who attacked the Capitol on January 6, 2021.

These Are More Than Differences

Kate

I think I'm supposed to forget and forgive.
To set aside differences and look for what makes us the same,
to reach for common ground, stay calm, keep it tame,
but this time I won't.
I can't.
These are more than differences.

This is right versus wrong.
This isn't my ideologies simply brushing against yours,
this isn't us wanting the same things but opening different doors,
this isn't us both singing, just different songs.
You are wrong.
These are more than differences.

There is no justification for denying justice.
You are not choosing the lesser of two evils.
You are choosing you and yours, before people;
you are following a mad man, to his lynchings of hate,
and it's not OK. It is not OK!
These are more than differences.

Wouldn't It Be Something

Nancy, Shawna (a conversation at Jack's)

Wouldn't it be something
If we listened to each other?
Not the fake I-want-to-respond type,
But the I-hear-you-and-heal-you type.
Let's-truly-rebuild-America type of listening.

Wouldn't it be something
If some of us listened to ourselves?
Not the convenient I-want-this-over-and-done type,
But the I'm-willing-to-be-wrong-to-make-you-right type.
Let's-truly-rebuild-America type of listening.

Wouldn't it be something
If we cried together?
Not out of frustration,
But the I-feel-your-pain-and-want-to-help-you tears.
The we-are-the-same-yet-just-figured-it-out tears.
The it's-sad-that-you-are-unsafe-in-your-community cry.
The I'm-on-bended-knee-for-you type of cry.

Wouldn't it be something
If we cried together?
Not out of anger or self-pity,
But the I-see-your-pain-and-my-hand-in-it tears.
The we-are-different-but-I-want-to-figure-out-all-I-don't-know tears.
The it's-wrong-that-you-are-unsafe-in-your-community-while-I'm-safe-in-mine cry.
The I'm-on-bended-knee-for-repentance-asking-forgiveness type of cry.

Wouldn't it be something
If we learned together?
Not the prove-we-are-right knowledge,
But the how-can-we-heal-and-unify-our-country knowledge.
The we-both-want-the-same-for-our-children-and-families knowledge.
The we-have-more-in-common-than-different type of learn,
So we can truly make America great.
Now wouldn't that be something?

Wouldn't it be something
If we learned together?
Not the prove-you-are-right knowledge,
But the tell-me-what-I-don't-know-and-should-have-asked knowledge.
The we-both-want-our-children-to-live-in-a-different-America knowledge.
The I-have-a-lot-of-work-to-do-and-I'm-sorry kind of learn,
So we can truly make America great for both of us. All of us.
Now wouldn't that be something?

Church and Politics

Gretchen (Sunday, January 10, 2021, *quoted scriptures taken from the *ESV* are cited in a final footnote.)

We sang about you.
    Of you,
      to you,
About building our lives
    upon "the cornerstone," our "firm foundation."
We sang of loving as you love.
We sang so loudly that we trust you, Jesus.
We sang so, so loud.

But do we?
Do we trust you like that?
Do we love as you love?

What would it look like?
Because I'm not sure I see it
when we're outside of this room,
when I'm straining my eyes to find goodness.
    To see you
        —in us.

Because we don't just shout here.

We shout outside at one another,
at those we other
    and those we dehumanize.
Are we standing upon your love then?
Are we shouting from a firm foundation?
Are we shouting as you shout?
Is that even a thing?

From what I remember,
loving as you love looks different.

It looks like touching the untouchable,
    unafraid

with your hands. [31]
It looks like writing silently,
    in the dirt
    waiting for the sinless to cast the first stone.[32]
It looks like all those stones dropping,
    heavy
    and useless,
    condemnation replaced by footprints in that dirt,
    retreating to repentance.
It looks like silence,
    walking to a cross
    amidst shouts for blood,
        and shouts of hate.
It looks like sacrifice, not shouting.
It's not so loud.

We also sang that we trust you, Lord,
but what do our words mean?

I imagine trust starts with knowing you.
That's how it usually begins.
That's how trust usually takes shape.
It's sitting across from someone
up close
getting to know them
and hearing their story.

Yet in the loud amphitheater outside this room,
the amphitheater we live in,
the amphitheater we have a voice in,
amidst all that shouting,
where are you to be found?
Oh, how much we need you!
To show us who you are.
To sit down beside us
and show us who we ought to be.

---

[31] *See* Matt. 8.
[32] *See* John 8.

Because so many claim to know,
as so many spew hate in your holy name.
And it stings.
Even when it's not aimed at me.

I'm protected
without consent, but by design.
I'm cloaked and hidden by privilege.
By labels like "Christian,"
and by money,
and by the power of just being White.
I suppose this cloak makes me lucky.
I know that it does.
I know that it has made my life easy,
even as I try desperately to tear it off.
Even though it makes me feel dirty,
and unclean,
and so, so far from pure.
Nothing like the "white as snow" I remember hearing about inside these walls.

Why?
Because, God, I'm struck by *your* words.
Because I cannot unhear them.
Because you lay me bare, with your truth.

Because
        ..."Blessed are the poor in spirit,
for theirs is the kingdom of heaven."
Because
        ..."Blessed are the meek,
for they shall inherit the earth."
Because
        ..."Blessed are the peacemakers,
for they shall be called [children] of God."

And I wonder,
Lord,
isn't THAT you?
Isn't that who Jesus really is?
Isn't that what love *actually* looks like?
Isn't that the true shape of the cornerstone,
the only firm foundation,
the Jesus we need to trust?

Yes.
But I still don't see you…in us…out there.
I don't think we're trusting you with our lives, Lord.
Not while we're all still shouting.

Church!
Where is
    not rich, not loud,
    but poor in spirit?
Church!
Where is
    not powerful, not proud,
    but humble and meek?
Church!
Where is
    not hateful, not self-righteous,
    no soapbox to stand on,
    no amphitheater required.
Where is peacemaking,
just peacemaking,
yes, the actual making of peace?

Church!
Where is
    loving, not othering?
Church!
Where is
    elevating the marginalized, not self?
Church!
Where is
    humanizing everyone,
    always—
    no matter who,
    no matter what?
Church!
Where is
    seeing dignity
    in every person,
    in every soul God made?

Where is displaying dignity
...in ourselves?

I know it's hard.
It's hard for me—
to build my life upon his love,
    to love as he loves,
      from his firm foundation,
    to really trust in Jesus.
It's hard.
But it's much less loud,
and it's much more good.

And I think that's how we find him,
outside.
That's how we see him
in us.
... "Blessed are the pure in heart,
      for they shall see God."

Oh Lord, help us see you,
    out there,
    in us.
Help us to stand in the light,
to step out of this loud,
    exhausting,
    filthy darkness,
and actually,
    finally,
    love as you love.
Actually look like Jesus,
    like your Church,
    your hands, your feet.[33]

---

[33] All scriptures quoted in this poem are taken from the *ESV*. Study Bible-ESV. English Standard Version, Crossway Bibles, 2014. ("the cornerstone" Ps. 118.22; "firm foundation" 2 Tim. 2.19; "white as snow" Is. 1.18; "Blessed are the ..." Matt. 5.3,5,8,9.)

Yeah, You Won the Vote

Aliyah (January 13, 2021, President Trump is impeached by the House for an unprecedented second time.)

Yeah, you won the vote!
Only president to have done so.
Popular vote was yours
TWICE, on the House floor.

Now you're readin' teleprompters,
lying and scared, looking' somber.
Suddenly your cash at stake,
no perks, no love, no place on stage.

Yeah, you won the vote!
Impeached, that speech, you gave to those,
who took your name and waved it high.
"We love you," so like hell go fight!

So, they trampled hope an' hist'ry,
Tryin' to eke out your false vict'ry.
Majority never made you their Joe.
Maybe Senate will impeach, by popular vote.

This Is America

Shawna

We need to stop saying
"This is not America."
It's a lie.
"This is not who we are."
It's a lie.
"All Lives Matter"
Black or Blue
Black or White
Deserve equal justice in her sight.
It's a lie.
Rich, poor, middle class,
Natural born, or immigrant
Are all welcome here.
It's a lie.

To know her is to love her.
To challenge her,
To push her towards greatness.
This is America.
Protests, speaking out
That's what makes her better.
Voting for change
Calling out injustice for Liberty's name.
Proud roots
Deep in Native soil.
Shores have seen it all
—Free and slave—
It's who we are.
This is America.

We are the land of the stolen,
Bought, refugee, invited,
The unseen, and unheard.
Rich and poor,
Prayed up, locked up,
Hopeful and homeless.
Left and right wing,
Judgmental and judged.

Protestors, rioters, looters,
And demonstrators.
Leaders and followers,
Challengers and incumbents.
This is America.

We are the land of party lines
And profit
Over people.
Of me too
And not you!
Red and blue,
Liberal and conservative,
The haves and have nots,
Anti-guns and gun toting,
Voting and non-voting,
Shut up and speak up.
This is America.

"This is not America,"
I hear you say.
"I wish everyone would just pray.
Let God have His way."
"Speak in kindness when we disagree"
What about freedom of religion
To believe or not believe?
What if to pray, we have to take a knee?
"Well, not at a football game or for equality."
Oh, now we're back to hypocrisy.
This is America.

Quiet Tonight

Shawna (January 16, 2020)

It's quiet tonight.
With no breaking glass,
No clashes,
Or shouting about liberals, media, insurrection, or coup,
Lost elections, or insurrection.
No screaming, no aggression.
No Covid and no vaccines.
It's quiet enough to hear my baby breathe.
Soft sighs escape her like all is right with the world.
For her, my innocent baby girl.
Maybe she'll see this time in history books.
Maybe hindsight will cause folks to take another look
At their actions, both pros and cons.
Challenge us to be better, each and every one.
But tonight, it's quiet tonight.
For her, my baby girl, everything is alright.

Callous Days

Will (January 17, 2021, the country is expected to pass 400,000 dead from Covid any day. Someone Will knows dies of cancer, and he is struck by how much death he has witnessed in a single year, in a single life. People who should still be walking around on this earth. He thinks of Son, of all the lost ones, and he mourns.)

Another one gone.
This time it wasn't Covid,
or riot.
It wasn't sudden or senseless.
It was death
and dying.
And there is nothing ordinary about it.

Have we forgotten?
The wrongness of death,
the bite, the gut punch of finality?
The brutality, the despair of loss?
The feeling of having
your heart ripped from your chest
and maimed,
then discarded because of time,
and its rules?
Because of its cruelty?

There's nothing natural about death.
That's just a lie people tell.
The world is full of lies
and liars.
When it should be full of
you.
Your body
walking around well.
Your light shining.

But your light is gone.
And it is unthinkable,
unimaginable.
This darkness is wrong!
Despicable!
And there's nothing ordinary about it.

Lord!
May we wake up and behold
all this dark, all this death.
All this tragic loss of light.
All this tragic loss of LIFE!
May we see death
as it truly is:
Unforgivable.
Unyielding.
Always remarkable,
and tragic.
Always wrong,
and unnatural.
Always, always, always
not as it was meant to be...

And may we
lament,
all this loss—
Black bodies in the street,
400,000 gone—
so much blood on our screens
on our hands,
drained from our souls—
all this death,
and dying.

May we lament,
and may we repent
    our hearts,
in these callous days.

Reflecting Pool

Mama (January 19, 2021, America passes 400,000 dead from Covid-19,
and the country watches a Memorial Service at the Capitol Reflecting Pool
on the eve of Inauguration Day.)

Holding my breath,

I stood locked in time.
The shores of those depths

Reflect

In the pools of my eyes.

400,000 have died!

Lord!

How many thousands have cried?

God!

How many Sons lost?
How many Daughters died?

Souls losing their breath.
Souls losing to time.

Lighted shores of their depths

Reflect

In the pools of our eyes.

Now

Imani

I've been mulling.
Writing angry poetry.
Lamenting buckets of tears.
Sitting long in the sun to feel its warmth,
even as this winter causes me to shiver.

Last May, I saw it coming.
Back when I still spoke of this place as only a possibility.
When I still hoped we would find our way back to civility.
Before George Floyd died. Before a nation stopped breathing.
Before…we never turned back, eyes open, choosing instead to stack, death upon
    death upon death.

No one's even running.
Fires keep lighting.
The glare too blinding to imagine horizons worth fighting
for. I still want more: Life, the death toll to stop climbing,
to feel hope again rising—defiant against night.

But is it unbecoming,
to lie to my heart when my eyes behold all this ash
in the air? All we've burned and keep burning, rash independence that flares,
persistently ignorant that when sacrifice is scarce…
it's freedom we burn, into this ash, in the air.

Is there anything we've learned?
Any goodness we didn't burn
into this ash,
in the air?

Light

I Sit in Light

Imani

I sit in stillness today.
Remembering yesterday
Not as a path to recede,
But as a tale to heed.
Willing the hope in my heart
To relish a new start
Of open mindedness,
Of healing and kindness,
Where my fellow man
Is first human.
I sit in light today.
Welcoming equality and justice,
Welcoming a new way to focus,
On unity
And an America of the free.

She Looks Like Me

Shawna (January 20, 2021, Inauguration Day, A conversation between Shawna and her daughter as they watch Amanda Gorman, National Youth Poet Laureate, redeem the power of words for all the world.)

She looks like me
Mama
Sunshine and bright
Mama
Her voice sounds like light
Mama
She is beautiful
Mama
I love her braids
Mama
She speaks of change
Mama
Could I be like her
Mama
Strong Black girl?

Mama smiled,
She didn't hold back tears
As she pondered how to answer her **daughter**.
The weight of this world etched on her face,
As she knelt down to her.
She placed her hand on her **daughter's** head
And drank in the hope in her eyes.

She looks like you
Daughter
Bright like dawn
Daughter
Casting light
Daughter
On a world still White
Daughter
And she is beautiful
Daughter
Braids like you
Daughter

Full of change *for* you
Daughter
You will stand tall like her
Daughter—
 and be your own—
Strong Black girl.

Wrapped in her **mama's** arms,
Daughter was known.
Mama wiped another tear
That escaped her tightly closed eyes.
Wondering when her beautiful Black girl
Would become the feared
ANGRY, BLACK WOMAN.
Mama wasn't ready for
The world
To see her baby as
The darkness.
When all she saw was light.
But could tomorrow be different?
Could **daughter** shine
Clothed in canary yellow prayers
And proclamations of a better dream?
Could empty promises and ideals
Be redeemed?
Because
"She looks like me, **Mama**"

Chucks and Pearls

Sisters (January 20, 2021, Inauguration Day, watching Kamala Harris, the first woman, and the first woman of color, become the Vice President of the United States.)

I've dreamed of it.
I've hoped for it.
I've even told my daughters and nieces about it.
This day. This day
When a woman of color
Would be there
Inducted as VP
In her Chucks and pearls.[34]
Skin, like mine.
Hair, like mine.
Smile, like mine.
Pride, like mine.
On every Black woman's face
And every little Black girl's face—
Awestruck
"She looks like me."

I dreamed of it.
I've hoped for it.
I voted for it!
Her presence symbolizing an era in our history,
Black History,
Women's History,
American History,
In her Chucks and pearls.
Skin, like mine.
Hair, like mine.
Smile, like mine.
Pride, like mine.
Representing me.

---

[34] In honor of Kamala Harris, women across the country wore Chucks (Converse All Stars) and pearls. Vice President Harris is known for wearing both. (*See* Nguyen, Andrew. "Why Are Women Wearing Chucks and Pearls Today?" *The CUT*, thecut.com, 20 Jan. 2021,
https://www.google.com/amp/s/www.thecut.com/amp/2021/01/women-wear-chucks-and-pearls-to-celebrate-kamala-harris.html. Accessed 20 Jan. 2021.)

A fulfillment of an American promise
I'd hoped to be true.
Astonished
"She looks like me."

I dreamed of it.
I've hoped for it.
I voted for it!
I bought the t-shirt for it!
Joined a Facebook group for it!
Draped myself in pearls
And bought new Chucks.
Readying myself to represent her as she represents me
And millions of women
In our Chucks and Pearls.
Skin, like mine.
Hair, like mine.
Smile, like mine.
Pride, like mine.
Paving a road of ambition and potential
I've prayed for.
Proud!
"She looks like me."

May God Bless America

Hope (January 20, 2021,
excerpts from President Joseph Biden's Inaugural Address)[35]

"A cry for racial justice some 400 years in the making moves us.
The dream of justice for all will be deferred no longer.

...

Let us listen to one another.

Hear one another.
See one another.

...

WE MUST END THIS UNCIVIL WAR.... .

...

Sustained by faith.

Driven by conviction.

...

May God bless America... ."

---

[35] Biden, Joseph. "Inaugural Address by President Joseph R. Biden, Jr." *WH.GOV*, The White House, 20 Jan. 2021, https://www.whitehouse.gov/briefing-room/.

Crash

Kate (January 20, 2021, Inauguration Day)

My heart in my throat,
My prayers in my eyes.
Can you give back to me
"Sweet land of liberty"?[36]
Could that really be hope
Crashing into my cries?
Can you give me back light,
"[O]ur flag…still there"[37] through the night?
Is that a woman I see?
Is that color on stage?
Can you promise real change,
A land for all, if we're brave?
Feel the fireworks' blast,
Crash your dreams into mine,
Can you make me believe
"[Y]our tired, your poor,…[will] breathe free"?[38]
Can you give back to me
All I dreamt my country could be?

[36] Smith, Samuel Francis. "America (My Country 'Tis of Thee)." 1832.
[37] Key, Francis Scott. "The Star-Spangled Banner." 14 Sept. 1814.
[38] Lazarus, Emma. "The New Colossus." Statue of Liberty. New York, NY 1883.

Deep and Real

Ty, Darius

*"I know the forces that divide us are **deep** and they are **real**."*[39]

(President Joseph Biden)

Ty

I've been sitting here listening to his words,
trying to believe in the possibility of change
that I've heard.
Trying to dig up this deep hurt
and distrust I feel.
Trying to find a way
to begin to heal
From what I experience daily
and from what I see.
I don't know if I can release these feelings
inside of me.
I don't know if I can let go of the years
of being treated less-than.
What makes now, this president, this country,
different from what it's been?

---

[39] Biden, Joseph. "Inaugural Address by President Joseph R. Biden, Jr." *WH.GOV*, The White House, 20 Jan. 2021, https://www.whitehouse.gov/briefing-room/.

Darius

Man, I hear you, and understand what you say.
And it reminds me of Mama, saying we need to pray.
Sometimes I think that his words, Mama's prayers,
are not enough.
But to heal, to move forward,
I have to trust.
And believe that our efforts, our marching, are not in vain.
I won't stop speaking out and my dignity, I will claim.
But I also won't carry the injustices in my heart.
I'm reclaiming hope
and Mama's prayers
for a new start.
I'll keep striving for equality and justice.
I won't let those divisive forces work against us.
I believe America is the land of the brave
and free.

...I can't say I don't have some hesitation,
but those words spoken at Biden's inauguration,
may be just what we all need,
to end this firestorm of hate and anger, *starting with me.*

Inauguration Day

Sisters

That day, January 20, 2016,
We dissented,
Decidedly different.
Thunder rumbled in the wake
Of divisiveness and doom.
We felt
Weighed down underneath an uncertain fate.
We cried.
4 years ago, through the streets,
We marched
Head up, arm in arm with purposeful strides.
We protested
Women, men, brothers, sisters, Black and White, gay and straight.
In tears and with signs,
We raised
our voices against hate.
A force of many
In disbelief and with common intention—
We lifted
our voices,
Decidedly disgruntled.

Today, on January 20, 2021,
We stand,
Decidedly different.
A hopeful hush hovering over us.
We weathered
A stormy season
of severed expectations of our leaders and countrymen.
We prevailed
Together.
Today, inviting unity, decency, and democracy,
We witnessed
Embraces, fist bumps, and a collective exhale as
Women, men, brothers, sisters, Black and White, gay and straight.
In tears and with signs,
We raised
our voices for unity.
A force of many
Hopeful and with common intention—
We lifted
our voices,
Decidedly different.

Openly Optimistic

Shawna, Aliyah, Imani (January 20, 2021, Inauguration Day)

Shawna

Openly optimistic,
A smile slid across my lips.
Tears glisten in my eyes,
Proud and poised,
Humble and honored
By our America.
Bruised, She may be—
Battered, but unbroken—
Changed yet resilient—
Determined and decidedly democratic—
Still America.

Aliyah

Openly optimistic,
Watching an inaugural celebration
With masked faces.
Socially distanced,
Yet eyes glistening with hope,
Of forging forward as a nation
With a new respect for democracy.
An American democracy,
Which promises that
We, the people,
American people,
Continue to strive to form a more perfect Union.
We are
Still America.

Imani

Openly optimistic,
Watching historic moments,
First moments,
Reunifying moments,
I'm openly optimistic,
And tearfully resigned to continue to hope
For Her growth.
America never promised perfection,
And we've witnessed Her struggle,
But I'm hopelessly optimistic
Because we are
Still America.

Epilogue

America's Future

You

You write what comes next.
Your voice matters now.

Share your creativity, your change, the power of your voice.

#uncivilwaramericanvoices

A Note From the Authors

Completing this book has taken sweat and tears. It has turned us upside down and inside out. But of all the tasks we had to complete, choosing a poem to end this work was the hardest. Oh how we wanted it to be *She Looks Like Me*! Such bright light seen through the eyes of youth; promising tomorrow could look different. We also strongly considered ending with the truth of *This is America*. Yes, America has seen change in 2020, and we have even seen triumph! But no, we are not there yet. We are not healed, and we are not OK.

In the end, we chose the resilient hope of *Openly Optimistic*. 2020 was a year that inflamed and singed the soul of a nation. Our characters, especially our Black voices, felt this in a deep, excruciating way. Yet—*we want desperately to believe*—that 2020 burned it all down, not so the ash could be trampled underfoot, and the old ways rebuilt, but instead, so new life could begin to grow from beneath this scorched earth.

But will it?

That all depends on you. It is our fervent hope that the American voices in this collection have made you feel something, learn something new, and maybe even begin to ask more questions—just as we have. But the question we need answered now is this: *What are you going to do next?* What are *you* going to do about all you've learned and all you still don't know?

What tools will *you* have in your hands to see the next part through? What are *you* willing to lay down, loosen, and untie? What are *you* willing to grab hold of, discover, and create? What are *you* willing *of you* to give, to lose, to unite, and to gain? And most importantly: *Who will you choose to be?*

We believe in you.

That may not mean much to you, but we wouldn't be here—risking our reputations, the backlash for our words, the lost relationships and hateful scorn—if it didn't mean something deep and vital to us. We also believe in beginnings, and we believe in change. Despite everything we have witnessed, we remain foolishly and doggedly hopeful in America and the power of American voices. Because we know, if we are going to end this uncivil war, we will first have to fight **in it**.

We have engaged in this fight though the book you hold in your hand. You have engaged in this fight by leaning in and listening to the voices within these pages. But the fight isn't over. It's time to end things that should have ended, grow things that should have grown, and fight battles that *must* be fought.

We'll be there fighting right beside you.

Together, let's take on the systems and bullies, the biases and hate, and all that has both insulated and guaranteed the survival of a two-caste racist system in America. *Together,* our American voices can turn meaningful change into reality. Because we have found within the flames of 2020, within the voices of America itself, a priceless thing—we have found a place to begin.

Let's not waste it.

About the Authors

Sister friend,
Your words have been
A balm for my soul,
Proof that color lines
Only exist if we draw them.
You've filled this isolation with broad strokes of love and acceptance.

Sister friend,
We've cried at injustices together.
Laughed at the idiocy of entitlement
And drank to equity and equality.
While fanning the flames of democracy and righteousness with our words.

Sister friend,
More similar we are to each other
Than those around us might see.
Never letting divisiveness dictate our humanity
For one another,
Or our love for each other.

Sister friend,
The days have been darkened by
Left and right, lies,
Death, so much death and sadness,
But I'm thankful
That you've painted our friendship
With broad strokes of cascading light.

Acknowledgments

(Because we could not thank them all, we thanked our immediate family and our beta-readers. There are so many others who have loved us through this process. To all of you, our deepest thanks. How loved, and uplifted we are!)

Sister friend, you know—
This book exists because we grow
friendship, much better than hate.
These woven words have kept us sane.
And I am PROUD of what we've done!
Also, astonished and terrified,
but because we've done this work *together*,
we'll see it through, unified.

Brion, so steady and sure
that we're not crazy to daily pour
our souls, into this dream and dreams,
of all America could be.
Our biggest fan, our constant help,
we've made it here 'cause you love well.
My husband, my partner, my fellow dreamer,
my babies' father, I'll need you forever.

Mom, my biggest cheerleader,
you do not write, but you don't need to,
to understand the daughter God gave you
must use a pen to think, to be true.
So, you stand ready, offering help,
constant support and so generous.
Providing me coffee, hot tea, and chocolate.
Thank you for raising a headstrong daughter.

Kelsey, daughter-rock and friend,
you believe, and like the wind,
you gently push, with strength and love,
until my more's at last enough.
Until I've carved out words of fire,
shining with *our* hope and truth.
My grounded beauty, all that you do
helped craft a work we're both proud of.

Annabelle, sweet poet soul,
you're still too young to read these pages.
Yet daughter, in your deep, blue eyes,
I see pools of words you keep inside.
I see understanding, I see *great* light,
you'll never question why I write.
And I'll never question *who* you are,
my beautiful daughter, God's shining star.

Alex, my son so brave,
you make sure, I'm good, I'm safe.
You guard the door, my heart, my dreams,
me on my toes you'll always keep.
You have my heart, you have my faith,
that's something this world could *never* change.
You use your soul to continually teach
that courage is choosing—*to be me.*

Juliette, my youthful JOY!
Your resilience leaves me astounded.
You're unflappable and keep me grounded.
You're glue and grit for those you love,
Your strength is happiness. You don't give up,
Hold nothing back, share every drop.
Let no one tell you, what you're not.
Be the change, for which we've fought.

Kamy, my littlest love
you're not so little anymore.
One foot here, one out the door,
but you'll never leave me, that's for sure.
My quiet strength, my future bright,
so easy to love, so easy to like.
I want to be the "me" you see—
powerful woman in your eyes.

My funny **James**, my handsome son,
you still fit snugly in my arms.
You've kept me hugged and safe from harm,
and always miss me, when I'm gone.

Still needing me in every way,
but you're my gentleman every day.
Opening my doors, my heart, my hope,
You say, "I love you," and make me know.

Tiffany, where do I start?
You've received so many texted drafts,
waves of poetry on you crashed,
some were good, and some were *trash!*
But you've encouraged to the last,
in the year without an end.
No matter your struggle, no matter your pain,
you always made space to be my friend.

Rachel, you lent your eye,
to the roughest version of collective cries.
You challenged our purpose,
you challenged our voice,
pushed us to make the narrow choice.
Asked the right questions,
and gave us courage,
to be real change, and not more noise.

Kristen, you read and read,
for my dreams, you'll always sacrifice,
your time, your eyes, your brilliant mind,
unparalleled friendship, unaffected by time.
I *always* miss you. Oh, how I miss you!
In every moment, in every way.
Yet somehow, you're here, my sister soul,
blessed friendship for all my days.

Kadena, my friend, my cousin,
you bring experience with your praise.
Help me navigate the publishing haze,
creating clarity for each new page,
of this journey, of this love we share.
As we reach and *dare* to believe,
we have something to say, contribute, and *be.*
Writers and cousins, kindred and free.

Lauren, you make life *fun!*
No matter the shit that hits the fan,
you choose to smile, to hope, to plan,
for when it's better, our feet in sand.
And you brought that spirit to this work!
Measured by your wise and thoughtful words.
You gave your all and gave your time,
to help make true these dreams of mine.

Clay, the lone male reader,
new to poetry, but not this fight.
New/old friend, from your insights,
we saw the holes, still left to write.
Hardworking and clearheaded,
an *honest* voice within this chaos,
who values character and integrity.
When I asked for your time, you did not hesitate.

Chevelle, you answered the call,
you clapped your hands, and doled out confidence.
Made me believe that this big land
might understand privilege and dominance.
I call your friendship God's great providence.
We carve out space, you help me walk in it.
And now you'll cheer me on in this!
Next steps are always best with friends.

Kyara, oldest friend,
please, move to Texas *right away!*
But how I'm grateful, that with a phone call,
time and distance get no say.
Too much history and *never judgement*,
means we only need to ask,
for an ear, a favor, wisdom,
you are the gift I'll *always* have.

Torrance, our cover artist,
and a friend from in my youth,
when we were green, and full of dreams,
idealists racing after truth.

You saw this book, you saw our vision,
and you captured it with lines
drawn with emotion, drawn with power,
the world now sees it through our eyes.

God, our Lord and Savior,
because you love us, we couldn't sleep
until the fire you made us to wield
came out as words of empathy.
You've seen our tears, you've held our hearts,
You've led us in this war-torn space,
where the oppressed, where Mama, where Son,
raise their voices in cries for change.

And you asked us both to write!
Against the hate, the lies, the silence.
You showed us your Kingdom, here on earth,
raises Black lives out of the margins.
You imbued the Psalms with light
Your heart for Justice and end to violence.
Asked us to trust You, with our lives,
telling your truth, can't be unrighteous.

At last, we thank **YOU**, Reader,
for trusting us with your time,
for taking a chance on a crazy idea,
allowing new voices into your life.
But it's your voice we're trusting now
to carry this dream beyond these pages.
You carry our heart, you carry the power,
to finish this war, when you're courageous.

WE THANK YOU!!!